Response to Intervention

RtI and CSI

Continuous School Improvement

Experts Bernhardt and Hebert's latest book demonstrates strategies to ensure your entire staff works together to design, implement, monitor, and evaluate a schoolwide prevention system with integrity and fidelity. Each step in this important resource is designed to help administrators, teachers, and other educators improve the learning of every student by implementing Response to Intervention (RtI) as part of a continuous school improvement process. This 2nd Edition spotlights the "Five Stages of RtI Implementation" and is complemented by the robust online RtI Implementation Guide, which includes more than 30 downloadable templates, examples, and other files to help schools start their journey of establishing a successful system. By applying the authors' insightful guidance in *Response to Intervention (RtI) and Continuous School Improvement (CSI),* you'll be able to redesign your general and special education programs to put your school on a path toward improvement!

Victoria L. Bernhardt, Ph.D., is Executive Director of the *Education for the Future Initiative,* a not-for-profit organization located at California State University, Chico, California, whose mission is to build the capacity of all learning organizations at all levels to gather, analyze, and use data to continuously improve learning for all students. She is also a Professor (currently on leave) in the College of Communication and Education, at California State University, USA.

Connie L. Hébert, M.S. Ed., is an experienced educator and consultant in the field of special education, and a K-12 Intervention Consultant for the Jackson R2 School District in Missouri, USA.

Response to Intervention

RtI and CSI

Continuous School Improvement

How to Design, Implement, Monitor, and Evaluate a Schoolwide Prevention System

2nd Edition

By
Victoria L. Bernhardt, Ph.D.
and Connie L. Hébert, M.S. Ed.

Second edition published 2017
by Routledge
711 Third Avenue, New York, NY 10017

and by Routledge
2 Park Square, Milton Park, Abingdon, Oxon, OX14 4RN

Routledge is an imprint of the Taylor & Francis Group, an informa business

First edition published by Routledge/Eye On Education 2011

Library of Congress Cataloging-in-Publication Data
Names: Bernhardt, Victoria L., author. | Hâebert, Connie L., author.
Title: Response to intervention and continuous school improvement : how to design, implement, monitor, and evaluate a schoolwide prevention system / by Victoria L. Bernhardt, Ph.D.and Connie L. Hâebert, M.S.
Other titles: Response to intervention (RTI) and continuous school improvement (CSI)
Description: Second edition. | New York : Routledge, 2017. | Includes bibliographical references and index.
Identifiers: LCCN 2016045464| ISBN 9781138285699 (Hardback) | ISBN 9781138285712 (Paperback) | ISBN 9781315268804 (Master) | ISBN 9781351977142 (Web PDF) | ISBN 9781351977135 (ePub) | ISBN 9781351977128 (mobipocket)
Subjects: LCSH: Learning disabled children--Education--United States. | Response to intervention (Learning disabled children)--United States. | Inclusive education--United States. | School improvement programs--United States. | School failure--United States--Prevention.
Classification: LCC LC4705 .B47 2017 | DDC 371.9--dc23
LC record available at https://lccn.loc.gov/2016045464

ISBN: 978-1-138-28569-9 (hbk)
ISBN: 978-1-138-28571-2 (pbk)
ISBN: 978-1-315-26880-4 (ebk)

Publisher's note: This book has been prepared from camera-ready copy provided by the authors.

Visit the companion website: www.routledge.com/cw/bernhardtandhebert

TABLE OF CONTENTS

ABOUT THE AUTHORS ix

PREFACE xi

ACKNOWLEDGEMENTS xv

1 RtI AND CSI: RESPONSE TO INTERVENTION AND
CONTINUOUS SCHOOL IMPROVEMENT 1

   RtI and CSI 2

   Stages of Implementation 3

      Stage 1: Study and Commit 5

      Stage 2: Plan 6

      Stage 3: Build Capacity 7

      Stage 4: Implement and Monitor 7

      Stage 5: Continuously Improve 8

   Book Study Questions...9

   Application Opportunities..9

2 RESPONSE TO INTERVENTION: STUDY AND COMMIT....................... 11

   Core Principles of RtI 15

   Intent of RtI 16

   Deficit Versus Risk Model 16

   Components of RtI 18

   Integrity and Fidelity of Implementation.......................................19

   Relationship of RtI to Special Education 20

   Book Study Questions..20

   Application Opportunities..20

3 CONTINUOUS SCHOOL IMPROVEMENT: STUDY AND COMMIT..........21

   Continuous School Improvement Framework 22

   Where Are We Now? 24

   Relationship of CSI to RtI..24

      Who Are We?...26

      How Do We Do Business? 27

      How Are Our Students Doing? 28

      What Are Our Processes?...29

      Looking Across the Multiple Measures of Data 29

How Did We Get to Where We Are? 30

Where Do We Want to Be? 30

How Are We Going to Get to Where We Want to Be? 31

Is What We Are Doing Making a Difference? 32

Book Study Questions..32

Application Opportunities...32

4 PLANNING WITH THE RtI IMPLEMENTATION GUIDE **33**

Planning with the RtI Implementation Guide 35

Components of the System of Responsive Interventions 39

Multi-Level Prevention System 46

Roles and Responsibilities 55

Referral Processes and Documentation 60

Other RtI Related Items for Which to Plan..61

Applying RtI to Behavior...61

Book Study Questions...62

Application Opportunities...62

5 BUILD CAPACITY **63**

Build Capacity 63

Leaders and Leadership Structures 64

Sharing with Staff 65

Professional Learning 65

Instructional Coherence 66

Parent Involvement 67

Book Study Questions...68

Application Opportunities...68

6 IMPLEMENT AND MONITOR **69**

Instructional Design for Primary Prevention 71

Instructional Design for Secondary and Tertiary Prevention.................................73

Data Teams for RtI 78

Documentation..83

Monitoring Implementation 84

Book Study Questions...86

Application Opportunities...86

7 RtI IMPLEMENTATION AND MONITORING TIMELINE..87

RtI Implementation and Monitoring Timeline...87

PATH Process...89

Book Study Questions...91

Application Opportunities..91

8 CONTINUOUSLY IMPROVE..93

Continuous School Improvement and Evaluation 93

Is RtI Being Implemented with Integrity and Fidelity?....................................93

Is Acceptable Progress Being Made?...96

What Is the Impact of RtI Implementation? 102

Book Study Questions..102

Application Opportunities...102

9 SUMMARY AND CONCLUSIONS...103

Stages of Implementation 104

What RtI Is Not...106

Recommendations...109

Book Study Questions..110

Application Opportunities...110

GLOSSARY 111

REFERENCES AND RESOURCES...123

INDEX...129

RtI IMPLEMENTATION GUIDE on accompanying website,
www.routledge.com/cw/bernhardtandhebert

ABOUT THE AUTHORS

VICTORIA L. BERNHARDT

Since 1991, Victoria L. Bernhardt, Ph.D., has directed the *Education for the Future Initiative,* a not-for-profit organization located at California State University, Chico, California, whose mission is to build the capacity of all learning organizations at all levels to gather, analyze, and use data to continuously improve learning for all students. She is also a Professor (currently on leave) in the College of Communication and Education, at California State University, Chico. Dr. Bernhardt is the author, or co-author, of the following books:

- *Data Analysis for Continuous School Improvement,* 3rd ed.
- *Creating Capacity for Learning and Equity in Schools: Instructional, Adaptive, and Transformational Leadership,* with Mary A. Hooper.
- *Shifting to Common Core Literacy: Reconceptualizing How We Teach and Lead,* with Cheryl Z. Tibbals.
- *From Questions to Actions: Using Questionnaire Data for Continuous School Improvement,* with Bradley J. Geise.
- *Data, Data Everywhere: Bringing All the Data Together for Continuous School Improvement,* 2nd ed.
- A four-book collection of using data to improve student learning—*Using Data to Improve Student Learning in Elementary Schools; Using Data to Improve Student Learning in Middle Schools; Using Data to Improve Student Learning in High Schools;* and *Using Data to Improve Student Learning across School Districts.*
- *The School Portfolio Toolkit: A Planning, Implementation, and Evaluation Guide for Continuous School Improvement,* and CD-Rom.
- *The School Portfolio: A Comprehensive Framework for School Improvement,* 2nd ed.

Dr. Bernhardt is passionate about her mission of helping all educators continuously improve student learning in their classrooms, their schools, their districts, and states by gathering, analyzing, and using data. She has made numerous presentations at professional conferences and conducts workshops on the school portfolio, data analysis, RtI and CSI, and continuous school improvement at local, state, regional, national, and international levels.

Dr. Bernhardt can be reached at:

Victoria L. Bernhardt, Ph.D.
Executive Director
Education for the Future Initiative
400 West First Street, Chico, CA 95929-0230
Tel: 530-898-4482
e-mail: vbernhardt@csuchico.edu
website: http://eff.csuchico.edu

CONNIE L. HÉBERT

Connie L. Hébert, M.S. Ed., is an experienced educator and consultant in the field of special education, currently working as a K-12 Intervention Consultant for the Jackson R2 School District in Jackson, Missouri. Previous experience includes work as special education teacher for students with cognitive disabilities, learning disabilities, emotional disturbance, autism, and multiple disabilities for school systems in five states. Connie left teaching to become a classroom-based consultant for twelve constituent school districts in Central Pennsylvania associated with the Central Intermediate Unit 10. Upon relocation to southeast Missouri, Connie became a systems level consultant for eighty plus school districts associated with the Southeast Regional Professional Development Center in Cape Girardeau.

In addition to working at the classroom level, Connie's background and experience has included assisting in the development and establishment of the Southeast Missouri State University Autism Center for Diagnosis and Treatment in 2007 where she remained as the founding director until 2014. Connie has been recognized for her expertise and contributions to the field of special education when named Missouri Staff Developer of the Year in 2005 and appointed to the Missouri Governor's Commission on Autism Spectrum Disorders from 2009 to 2014.

Connie also works as an independent consultant from her personal business, here2help, LLC, to provide services to school districts in many areas, including the development of systems of Response to Intervention. She has worked with systems level data analysis for continuous improvement since 2003, and has worked as an Associate with *Education for the Future* at the annual Summer Data Analysis and School Improvement Institutes. Schools that work with Connie find her approach to be student focused while remaining sensitive to the responsibilities of teaching in today's classroom. She is enthusiastic about supporting schools in the use of proven practices for effectively addressing the needs of students while meeting the expectations of federal and state legislation or other mandates as they relate to school improvement.

Connie can be reached at:

Connie L. Hébert
Independent Consultant
here2help, LLC
Cape Girardeau, MO
Tel: 573-450-6997
e-mail: connie.here2help@gmail.com

PREFACE

We are very excited to present to you the second edition of *Response to Intervention and Continuous School Improvement: How to Design, Implement, Monitor, and Evaluate a Schoolwide Prevention System.* Since the publication of the first edition, we have worked hard to make a text that would help any school with the design, implementation, monitoring, and evaluation of a schoolwide prevention system.

Schoolwide prevention systems have been called by various names, but are primarily known as systems for Response to Intervention (RtI) or Multi-Tier Systems of Support (MTSS). These terms are defined similarly in research and referenced similarly in legislation. Some sources describe distinct differences in these two terms, indicating MTSS to be a more comprehensive or inclusive model. Other sources use these or similar terms interchangeably since they do share similar foundations, origins, and components. Regardless of what a multilevel prevention system may be called, schools continue to struggle to implement practices systemically, with fidelity. This edition provides guidance, tools, and resources for schools and districts to build a multi-level prevention system and implement that system with fidelity and integrity. We use the term RtI, referring to more than just a pyramid – more than just academics or behavior. We use the term RtI to reflect a system inclusive of *all* student learning needs, developing academic and social competence across every level of performance and ability.

Purposes of This Book

The purposes of *Response to Intervention (RtI) and Continuous School Improvement (CSI): How to Design, Implement, Monitor, and Evaluate a Schoolwide Prevention System* (2nd ed.) are to:

1. Describe a Continuous School Improvement (CSI) framework that will help schools redesign general and special education to implement a schoolwide prevention system.

2. Define RtI and its essential components.

3. Communicate 5 Stages of RtI Implementation.

4. Provide tools to help schools design, implement, monitor, and evaluate their systems of RtI.

5. Provide strategies and tools to help teams get all staff on the same page and moving forward together.

New in This Edition

Since the publication of *Response to Intervention (RtI) and Continuous School Improvement (CSI): Using Data, Vision, and Leadership to Design, Implement, and Evaluate a Schoolwide Prevention System,* (1st ed.), the authors have worked with hundreds of schools to design, implement, monitor, and evaluate their systems of RtI.

This work has made us smarter and eager to make this daunting task easier for all schools. We will never say we can make RtI easy, because it is not easy to put a comprehensive system in place.

However, we can help you think through and plan for all the elements that need to be defined and implemented. We can also share what we know about pitfalls along the way.

In *Response to Intervention (RtI) and Continuous School Improvement (CSI): How to Design, Implement, Monitor, and Evaluate a Schoolwide Prevention System, Second Edition,* we share an RtI Implementation Guide that helps schools define the details for all the components for RtI. The RtI Implementation Guide is used in discussion of RtI components in the chapters. The Guide appears in total, in downloadable and modifiable form, on the accompanying website, http://www. routledge.com/cw/bernhardtandhebert.

This edition has a new subtitle that emphasizes its practical focus – *How to Design, Implement, Monitor, and Evaluate a Schoolwide Prevention System.* At the end of each chapter are Book Study Questions and Application Opportunities. Staff can follow and implement the application opportunities to develop their own system of RtI, using the RtI Implementation Guide.

Intended Audience
The intended audiences for this book are:

1. School and school district administrator-teacher teams working to integrate general education and special education to continuously improve their learning organizations by designing and implementing robust prevention systems for RtI.

2. College professors and students learning about CSI and RtI design, implementation, monitoring, and evaluation in schools.

3. School staff book study groups. This book can help staff design, start, monitor, troubleshoot, and evaluate their own efforts for CSI and RtI implementation.

4. District administrator book study groups. This book can help district administrators think about CSI and RtI implementation from the perspective of the schools, and help them create systems in which all their schools can thrive.

5. Leadership Training Programs that are teaching about the impact strong leadership has on the implementation of CSI and RtI in schools.

Structure of This Book
Chapter 1, RtI and CSI: Response to Intervention and Continuous School Improvement, defines RtI and describes the *5 Stages of RtI Implementation.*

Chapter 2, Response to Intervention: Study and Commit reviews the concept and intent of *Response to Intervention (RtI)* and addresses the common components in implementing a comprehensive, responsive, evidence and research-based instruction and assessment system.

Chapter 3, Continuous School Improvement: Study and Commit provides a framework for reviewing where the school is now, for creating and implementing a shared vision, and for measuring the impact the vision and implementation strategies have on student achievement. A solid CSI foundation is the logical way to begin the design of a schoolwide system of prevention to improve the learning of *every* student. This chapter shows why CSI supports the creation of systems for RtI.

Chapter 4, Planning with the RtI Implementation Guide guides readers through the design of a system for Response to Intervention, complete with tools, templates, and examples to assist with specifying the many details.

Chapter 5, Build Capacity addresses a make-it-or-break-it component of systems for RtI – getting staff knowledgeable and committed to implementing with *integrity and fidelity.*

Chapter 6, Implement and Monitor provides structures that assist RtI designers with pulling the details together to implement with *integrity and fidelity.* These same structures can be used to monitor the implementation of systems for RtI.

Chapter 7, RtI Implementation and Monitoring Timeline is devoted to laying out a plan for the annual implementation of a schoolwide prevention system by looking at activities necessary to complete before school starts, as school begins, throughout the school year, in the middle of the year, and as the year ends.

Chapter 8, Continuously Improve provides suggestions for using data to evaluate RtI to know if your processes and interventions are making the differences you want to see in every classroom, in every grade level, and in every subject area.

Chapter 9, Summary and Conclusions pulls together concepts from the eight previous chapters to provide guidance and logical considerations for getting started with designing, implementing, monitoring, and evaluating a system of RtI, using continuous school improvement. In addition, intended and unintended changes in the school that might result with RtI implementation are discussed.

www.routledge.com/cw/bernhardtandhebert houses the **RtI Implementation Guide** complete with tools and templates that are adjustable and downloadable, with examples. Schools can use the **RtI Implementation Guide** to design, implement, monitor, and evaluate their system of RtI and PBIS.

Book Study Questions at the end of each chapter are designed to engage individuals in the content of the chapter and to promote conversations about chapter content that will lead to the application of new ideas throughout the school.

Application Opportunities at the end of each chapter are designed to help RtI Design Teams establish successful Schoolwide Prevention Systems. A team can follow the chapters and

Application Opportunities to design, implement, monitor, and evaluate their system of RtI.

A comprehensive Glossary is provided at the end of the book to define the terms used in the chapters, and in RtI and CSI in general.

Written in a conversational style, *RtI and CSI* is firmly based on research and practice. The References and Resources section lists some of the many references and resources used to write this book and assist schools with designing, implementing, monitoring, and evaluating RtI. The authors strongly recommend these resources for deeper understanding.

We know you are going to love the new edition, especially the RtI Implementation Guide. We do. All our best to you as you design, implement, monitor, and evaluate your system of Response to Intervention.

ACKNOWLEDGEMENTS

Many people have contributed to making this second edition a valuable resource for educators to use in the design, implementation, monitoring, and evaluation of a system for Response to Intervention (RtI) using Continuous School Improvement (CSI). Numerous educators in school buildings, districts, complexes, state departments of education, colleges and universities have provided feedback and refinements for the RtI Implementation Guide included with this second edition.

We are extremely grateful to these people and to colleagues who work closely with us at *Education for the Future,* keeping us moving forward and striving for continuous improvement ourselves. This includes very special associate Joy Rose, who lends her communication and leadership expertise to make sure we create a clear and comprehensive understanding of the systems for RtI and CSI. It also includes Mary Younie who, expertly and quickly, laid out the contents of the book and the RtI Implementation Guide and patiently worked through the multiple edits. Additionally, we appreciate Heather Jarrow for her continuous support and guidance through the publishing maze.

Reviewers listed below provided critical suggestions, thoughts, and feedback as we finalized information and tools for both the book and the RtI Implementation Guide. Each reviewer provided attention to detail while holding us accountable for realities associated with the implementation of RtI in the field. We are deeply appreciative of the experience, knowledge, and skills they were willing to share in their reviews.

Amy Bartlow
Instructor
Teaching and Leadership
College of Education
Pittsburg State University
Pittsburg, KS

Beth Emmendorfer
Assistant Superintendent
Jackson R2 Schools
Jackson, MO

Brad Geise
Director of Questionnaire Services
Education for the Future
Chico, CA

Sowmya Kumar
Assistant Superintendent
Office of Special Education Services
Houston Independent School District
Houston, TX

Kathy Miller
Executive Director of Instructional Services
and Secondary Options
MERA Board President
Henderson, MI

Derek Minakami
Principal
Kāne'ohe Elementary School
Kāne'ohe, HI

Carol Reimann
Literacy Specialist and Consultant
Southeast Regional Professional
Development Center
Southeast Missouri State University
Cape Girardeau, MO

Joy Rose
Retired Administrator
Westerville, OH

Louise Stearns
Senior Lecturer, Curriculum and Instruction
College of Education and Human Services
Southern Illinois University
Carbondale, IL

Michael Webb
Senior Manager Child Study
Office of Special Education Services
Special Education Field Office
Houston Independent School District
Houston, TX

Diane Yoshimura
Data Governance Office
Hawaii Department of Education
Honolulu, HI

Participants in our RtI Institutes

Finally, we thank our family members who support this work in ways expected and unexpected, and who endure our time away from home which allows us to provide ongoing support to schools, nationally and internationally. We love you for your encouragement to continue, reminding us of the outcomes systems achieve based on the training and resources we provide.

To our readers — thank you for your commitment to improving teaching and learning for all who have the privilege to work and learn in education at all levels.

Victoria Bernhardt and Connie Hébert

CHAPTER 1

RtI and CSI:
Response to Intervention and
Continuous School Improvement

*Until you get continuous school improvement right, you cannot
get RtI right. If you do continuous school improvement right,
you will have a good start toward an effective RtI system.
If you do RtI right, you will be engaged in a
continuous school improvement process.*

Victoria L. Bernhardt and Connie L. Hébert

Response to Intervention (RtI) refers to a comprehensive and deliberate *system* of implementing and monitoring responsiveness to interventions using multiple levels of instruction and assessment designed by schools to address the learning needs of *all* students. RtI encourages intervening early to prevent student failure and to ensure academic success and positive behavior, while reducing the likelihood that students are wrongly identified for special education services. RtI is defined by the National Center on Response to Intervention as follows:

> *Response to intervention integrates assessment and intervention within a multi-level prevention system to maximize student achievement and reduce behavior problems. With RtI, schools use data to identify students at risk for poor learning outcomes, monitor student progress, provide evidence-based interventions and adjust the intensity and nature of those interventions depending on a student's responsiveness, and identify students with learning disabilities or other disabilities. (www.RtI4success.org)*

Significant redesign of general education and special education is required for a school or school district to implement RtI and to improve the learning of all students. Adding a program or intervention, here or there, will not provide the improvement which schools desire or require to meet the learning needs of all students.

Significant redesign of general education and special education is required for a school or school district to implement RtI and to improve the learning of *all* students. Adding a program or intervention, here or there, will not provide the improvement which schools desire or require to meet the learning needs of *all* students.

Continuous School Improvement (CSI) is the process of improving an organization on an ongoing basis. CSI involves:

◆ analyzing all types of data to understand where the school is now,

◆ understanding how the school is getting its current results,

◆ clarifying where the school wants to go,

◆ determining how the school will get to where it wants to go,

◆ implementing the processes to take the school where it wants to go,

◆ evaluating the parts and the whole, on an ongoing basis, to know if the parts are effective and aligned to where the school wants to go, and

◆ improving the parts and the whole on an ongoing basis.

CSI provides the paradigm shift for all staff members that implementing RtI requires.

CSI provides the paradigm shift for all staff members that implementing RtI requires.

As a method for schools to rethink general and special education and to avoid piecemeal change, CSI processes facilitate the design, implementation, monitoring, and evaluation for systems of RtI.

When schools establish systems of RtI through CSI processes, staff get the system and commitments in place before specific strategies.

School staff members who start RtI at the whole school level using a CSI framework understand what their students know and do not know. These staff members make agreements and commitments to get *all* students on grade level with direct, intense core curriculum supported with intensive and focused interventions, even when that means moving some students more than one grade level in one year. When schools establish systems of RtI through CSI processes, staff get the system and commitments in place before specific strategies.

School staff members who start RtI at the individual student level assess the students and then think about interventions, sometimes coming to dead ends when they realize they cannot possibly do all the interventions they deem necessary. If schools implement RtI "right," they will unavoidably become engaged in continuous school improvement processes.

RtI and CSI

Response to Intervention (RtI) and Continuous School Improvement (CSI): How to Design, Implement, Monitor, and Evaluate a Schoolwide Prevention System is a guidebook for using Continuous School Improvement to develop a schoolwide prevention system, commonly known as Response to Intervention, that will ensure every students' success, and one that is implemented and monitored with *integrity and fidelity. Implementation* is putting a plan, process, or program into effect; *implementation with integrity* is putting a plan, process, or program into effect with accuracy and consistency. *Implementation with fidelity* is carrying out that plan, process, or program the way it is intended to be implemented. *Monitoring* of implementation is observing and checking routinely and systematically to address issues and provide support to ensure integrity and fidelity for optimal outcomes.

Stages of Implementation

RtI and CSI is organized with **Stages of RtI Implementation** in mind.

Stage 1: Study and Commit
Stage 2: Plan
Stage 3: Build Capacity
Stage 4: Implement and Monitor
Stage 5: Continuously Improve

The stages are shown in Figure 1.1 and are described on the next page.

Stages of Implementation

♦ *Stage 1: Study and Commit*

♦ *Stage 2: Plan*

♦ *Stage 3: Build Capacity*

♦ *Stage 4: Implement and Monitor*

♦ *Stage 5: Continuously Improve*

Figure 1.1
Stages of RtI Implementation

STAGE 1	STAGE 2	STAGE 3	STAGE 4	STAGE 5
Study and Commit	**Plan**	**Build Capacity**	**Implement and Monitor**	**Continuously Improve**

◆ All staff agree that *every* student can learn and be proficient, and deserves the opportunity to learn.
 	
◆ All staff conduct a school needs assessment, to help understand why RtI is necessary, which adds a sense of urgency.
 	
◆ All staff study structures and best practices with respect to RtI to build early ownership and understanding.
 	
◆ All staff create a clear shared mission and vision for the school.
 	
◆ All staff agree on a purpose of RtI for the school.
 	
◆ All staff agree on an RtI model that eliminates the needs uncovered in the needs assessment.
 	
◆ All staff agree to put RtI in place, with integrity and fidelity.
 	
◆ All staff determine system and policy implications of implementing RtI in the school.
 	
◆ All staff commit to collaborate for the best outcomes for students.
 	
◆ All staff understand factors that contribute to an inverted triangle and agree to levels of intervention and instruction that will exist in Primary Prevention.
 	
◆ All staff participate in ongoing professional learning.
	◆ Define each component of the schoolwide prevention system.
	
	◆ Design your school's multi-level prevention system.
	
	◆ Adopt universal screener and progress monitoring tools and develop processes for implementation.
	
	◆ Define roles and responsibilities of all stakeholders.
	
	◆ Develop plans for implementation, professional learning, and evaluation.
	
	◆ Reallocate resources to support RtI implementation.
	
	◆ Create policies, procedures, and guidelines.
	
	◆ Perform an "audit" of existing assessment and curricular materials and, if necessary, acquire or eliminate assessments and materials that are duplicative or do not support RtI outcomes and vision.
	
	◆ Build teachers' "toolbox" for improving existing instruction and for addressing intervention needs.
	
	◆ Provide ongoing professional learning.
		◆ Enlist all staff in committing to RtI, with integrity and fidelity.
		
		◆ Establish expectations for all staff.
		
		◆ Provide ongoing professional learning to understand and implement the system of RtI.
		
		◆ Provide ongoing professional learning related to effective instruction and intervention for your students.
		
		◆ Refine how different roles and responsibilities for all staff work together.
		
		◆ Inform and enlist parents, community, and other stakeholders regarding the benefits of the system of RtI.
		
		◆ Ensure commitment to implement, with integrity and fidelity, the system of RtI, with appropriate resources.
			◆ Deliver RtI components with integrity and fidelity.
			
			◆ Monitor RtI components for implementation integrity, fidelity, and outcomes.
			
			◆ Establish, monitor, and refine procedures and guidelines.
			
			◆ Provide ongoing professional learning for continued instructional improvement.
			
			◆ Integrate systemic data-informed decision making by reviewing:
			  • Universal screening data
			  • Progress monitoring data
			  • High quality preventive core instruction
			  • High quality evidence-based strategic interventions
			  • High quality evidence-based intensive interventions
			  • Monitoring and evaluation data for implementation with integrity and fidelity
			  • Monitoring and evaluation of outcomes
				◆ Conduct ongoing evaluations of the impact of RtI on individual student learning growth.
				
				◆ Conduct ongoing evaluations to monitor the integrity and fidelity of implementation.
				
				◆ Refine the plan, policies, and procedures based on observations, collaborative meetings, data analysis, parent input, and other monitoring data.
				
				◆ Determine if acceptable progress is being made.
				
				◆ Identify desirable practices to keep, and undesirable practices to eliminate.
				
				◆ Provide ongoing professional learning opportunities and support.
				
				◆ Monitor and address changes needed to ensure sustainability.
				
				◆ Evaluate outcomes.

Stage 1: Study and Commit

The *Study and Commit* stage sets the tone for system design and implementation. Stakeholders need to be a part of discovering why RtI is needed and how it will be designed and carried out. Effective leadership is required to create momentum for the study, commitment, development, and implementation of RtI, making this beginning stage extremely important.

The purposes of Stage 1: Study and Commit are to:

- ◆ analyze schoolwide multiple measures of data to understand why RtI is needed,
- ◆ review literature to study best practices and what research demonstrates RtI can do for the school,
- ◆ explore structures to implement, and
- ◆ obtain staff agreement and commitment to move forward with planning for RtI.

If your school is engaged in continuous school improvement, schoolwide data analysis and staff involvement will be natural.

Stage 1 Key Activities:

- ◆ All staff agree that *every* student can learn and be proficient, and deserves the opportunity to learn.
- ◆ All staff conduct a school needs assessment, to help understand why RtI is necessary, which adds a sense of urgency.
- ◆ All staff study structures and best practices with respect to RtI to build early ownership and understanding.
- ◆ All staff create a clear shared mission and vision for the school.
- ◆ All staff agree on a purpose of RtI for the school.
- ◆ All staff agree on an RtI model that eliminates the needs uncovered in the needs assessment.
- ◆ All staff agree to put RtI in place, with *integrity and fidelity.*
- ◆ All staff determine system and policy implications of implementing RtI in the school.
- ◆ All staff commit to collaborate for the best outcomes for students.
- ◆ All staff understand factors that contribute to an inverted triangle and agree to levels of intervention and instruction that will exist in *Primary Prevention.*
- ◆ All staff participate in ongoing professional learning.
- ◆ Provide ongoing professional learning.

Purposes of Stage 1: Study and Commit

- ◆ *analyze schoolwide multiple measures of data to understand why RtI is needed,*
- ◆ *review literature to study best practices and what research demonstrates RtI can do for the school,*
- ◆ *explore structures to implement, and*
- ◆ *obtain staff agreement and commitment to move forward with planning for RtI.*

If your school is engaged in continuous school improvement, schoolwide data analysis and staff involvement will be natural.

Stage 2: Plan

Research has shown that if schools do not have clear processes and procedures, they are *unlikely* to achieve desired outcomes. Some sites fail to plan, or they move too quickly through the planning process. Poor planning can lead to frustrated administrators and teachers, wasted resources, ineffective implementation, and little-if-any positive impact on student learning outcomes.

By establishing infrastructure and proper supports prior to implementation, sites are more likely to experience fuller practitioner and community support, more efficient use of resources, and more timely student benefit.

The purposes of Stage 2: Plan are to develop *clear plans, processes, and procedures for RtI* and to construct the *infrastructure and structural supports* necessary for successful RtI implementation.

Stage 2 Key Activities:

♦ Define each component of the schoolwide prevention system.

♦ Design your school's multi-level prevention system.

♦ Adopt universal screener and progress monitoring tools and develop processes for implementation.

♦ Define roles and responsibilities of all stakeholders.

♦ Develop plans for implementation.

♦ Develop plans for professional learning.

♦ Develop plans for evaluation.

♦ Reallocate resources to support RtI implementation.

♦ Create policies, procedures, and guidelines.

♦ Perform an "audit" of existing assessment and curricular materials and, if necessary, acquire or eliminate assessments and materials that are duplicative or do not support RtI outcomes and vision.

♦ Build teachers' "toolbox" for improving existing instruction and for addressing intervention needs.

♦ Provide ongoing professional learning in all stages.

Stage 3: Build Capacity

To have RtI implemented with *integrity and fidelity,* all staff must understand why the school is adopting RtI structures and processes, learn the purpose and components of RtI, and commit to implementing with integrity and fidelity.

The purpose of Stage 3: Build Capacity is to bring all components of the system for RtI into clarity so that it is:

- Embraced by all staff.
- Integrated into the system of how the school operates.
- Implemented with integrity and fidelity in every classroom.

Stage 3 Key Activities:

- Enlist all staff in committing to RtI, with *integrity and fidelity.*
- Establish expectations for all staff.
- Provide ongoing professional learning to understand and implement the system of RtI.
- Provide ongoing professional learning related to effective instruction and intervention for your students.
- Refine how different roles and responsibilities for all staff work together.
- Inform and enlist parents, community, and other stakeholders regarding the benefits of the system of RtI.
- Ensure commitment to implement, with *integrity and fidelity,* the system of RtI, with appropriate resources.

Stage 4: Implement and Monitor

Full operation of RtI occurs when the system of RtI is embraced by staff, integrated into all classrooms with *integrity and fidelity,* and embedded within all practices. *Stage 4: Implement and Monitor* is where the rubber meets the road.

When RtI is fully implemented, it becomes the way business is done and is woven into the culture of the school. Staff become skilled in data-informed decision making: Administrators and leaders support and facilitate new practices; procedures and processes are routine; community members understand and accept the system; and expected outcomes are clear. Instruction is evidence-based and culturally responsive. It is important to remember that significant changes in student achievement are unlikely to be seen until all components of RtI are fully implemented with *integrity and fidelity.*

*To have RtI implemented with **integrity and fidelity,** all staff must understand why the school is adopting RtI structures and processes, learn the purpose and components of RtI, and commit to implementing with integrity and fidelity.*

Purpose of Stage 3: Build Capacity

Bring all components of the system for RtI into clarity, so that it is:

- *Embraced by all staff.*
- *Integrated into the system of how the school operates.*
- *Implemented with integrity and fidelity in every classroom.*

*Full operation of RtI occurs when the system of RtI is embraced by staff, integrated into all classrooms with **integrity and fidelity,** and embedded within all practices.*

*...significant changes in student achievement are unlikely to be seen until all components of RtI are fully implemented with **integrity and fidelity.***

Purpose of Stage 4: Implement and Monitor

◆ *Set RtI into action with integrity and fidelity.*

The purpose of **Stage 4: Implement and Monitor** is to set RtI into action with *integrity and fidelity.*

Stage 4 Key Activities:

◆ Deliver RtI components with *integrity and fidelity.*

◆ Monitor RtI components for implementation *integrity and fidelity,* and outcomes.

◆ Establish, monitor, and refine procedures and guidelines.

◆ Provide ongoing professional learning for continued instructional improvement.

◆ Integrate systemic and systematic data-informed decision making by reviewing:

  ○ Universal screening data

  ○ Progress monitoring data

  ○ High quality preventive core instruction

  ○ High quality evidence-based strategic interventions

  ○ High quality evidence-based intensive interventions

  ○ Monitoring and evaluation data for implementation with integrity and fidelity

  ○ Monitoring and evaluation of outcomes

Stage 5: Continuously Improve

Effective schools continuously strive to improve practices to achieve better outcomes for students.

Effective schools continuously strive to improve practices to achieve better outcomes for students. *Stage 5: Continuously Improve* ensures that the system of RtI remains relevant to the needs of the school. During this stage, schools intensify their focus on activities they've done within all stages, evaluate their progress, adjust practices based on continuous evaluation, and monitor changes to ensure sustainability of RtI. Innovative practices may be introduced to enhance the match between the system of RtI and the evolving needs of students and teachers.

Purposes of Stage 5: Continuously Improve

◆ *Ensure the sustainability of RtI.*

◆ *Adjust the system of responsiveness to interventions for better serving student needs.*

◆ *Evaluate implementation* **integrity, fidelity, and outcomes.**

The purposes of **Stage 5: Continuously Improve** are to innovate and evaluate in order to improve practices to achieve better outcomes for *every* student by:

◆ Ensuring the sustainability of RtI.

◆ Adjusting the system of responsiveness to interventions for better serving student needs.

◆ Evaluating implementation *integrity, fidelity, and outcomes.*

Stage 5 Key Activities:

◆ Conduct ongoing evaluations of the impact of RtI on individual student learning growth.

◆ Conduct ongoing evaluations to monitor the *integrity and fidelity* of implementation.

◆ Refine the plan, policies, and procedures based on observations, collaborative meetings, data analysis, parent input, and other monitoring data.

◆ Determine if acceptable progress is being made.

◆ Identify desirable practices to keep, and undesirable practices to eliminate.

◆ Provide ongoing professional learning opportunities and support.

◆ Monitor and address changes needed to ensure sustainability.

◆ Evaluate outcomes.

Schools that invest the time and energy to design and implement RtI *right* find it beneficial for *every* student's learning growth. Developing and sustaining such a preventive, corrective, and supportive system requires investment of energy and resources. RtI can rejuvenate the passion that brought educators to the field to begin with – and with passion comes energy.

RtI can rejuvenate the passion that brought educators to the field to begin with – and with passion comes energy.

Book Study Questions

1. What are the Stages of RtI Implementation?

2. Why is it important to know the Stages of RtI Implementation?

Application Opportunities

1. Does your school currently have a system for Response to Intervention in place?

2. Why is your school establishing a system for Response to Intervention?

3. As you begin this journey, think about what your school does to help students who are not proficient. What does your school do to accelerate students who are proficient? How successful are these efforts? How do you measure the success of these efforts?

CHAPTER 2

Response to Intervention:
Study and Commit

---

*The purpose of RtI is not to prevent special education.
Rather, its twin aims are to prevent serious, long-term negative
consequences associated with exiting school without adequate
academic competence and to identify children with disabilities.
So, RtI is very ambitious in intent and scope.
Doing RtI right is not for the faint of heart. It will require
commitment, energy, teamwork, and smarts. But the potential
payoff of doing it right is large.*

Dr. Doug Fuchs and Dr. Lynn Fuchs
(Responsiveness to Intervention, 2009)

RtI includes a multi-level prevention *system* designed to address the
learning needs of *every* student with interventions provided as *each* student
demonstrates a need. RtI seeks to prevent student failure through coherent,
research-based instruction with frequent on-going assessment and progress
monitoring to inform instruction. Increasingly intensive levels of evidence-
based early interventions are provided for students who demonstrate risk
for poor learning outcomes. Students who do not respond positively to
continued or intensive interventions may become candidates for special
education evaluation.

RtI is a system for –

- Screening all students using valid, reliable, accurate measures to
  determine which students are at risk for poor learning outcomes.

- Providing multiple levels of evidence-based, culturally responsive
  instruction and early intervention to meet the specific needs of
  students.

- Monitoring progress within each intervention level to assist in
  determining the effectiveness of instruction and interventions, to
  adjust as necessary.

◆ Analyzing and utilizing data from multiple sources to inform decisions for designing systems of instruction and support that will lead to improved student outcomes.

Figure 2.1 is the National Center on Response to Intervention's representation of these components reflecting the interrelated, dynamic nature of the essential elements. (Retrieved from www.rti4success.com June 5, 2016.)

Figure 2.1
The System of Response Interventions

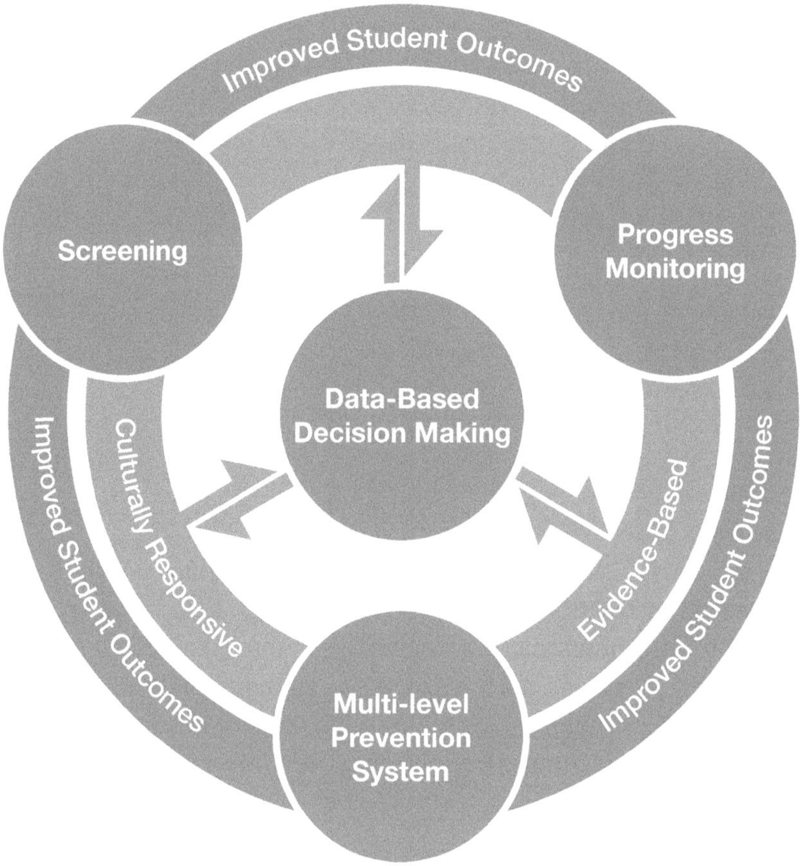

Conceptually, the structure for RtI has been around for some time and is being implemented in many places very effectively. The term Multi-Tier System of Support (MTSS) has been introduced as a means to communicate implementation of a "comprehensive" model that encompasses academic and behavioral or social/emotional aspects of prevention and early intervention. The way we define RtI is not different from the way MTSS proponents define MTSS. It is a *system* of early detection and prevention, which also accelerates students already achieving. We believe CSI and RtI, together, can achieve all that MTSS implies.

Schools engaged in Continuous School Improvement have in place many structures and processes that support implementation of RtI components, including high quality core instruction, assessments that inform instruction, mission, vision, leadership, and collaborative structures that enhance the analysis and utilization of data from multiple sources to inform decisions. For these schools, the work of establishing a system of RtI involves creating and maintaining a schoolwide prevention system and adequately documenting student responsiveness to multiple interventions to be used to support special education eligibility determinations, if needed.

Schools engaged in Continuous School Improvement have in place many structures and processes that support implementation of RtI components.

Figure 2.2 illustrates the multi-level prevention system associated with RtI as a three level triangle or pyramid graphic. The pyramid graphic shows dotted lines with the *Secondary and Tertiary Prevention Levels* being nested inside the *Primary Prevention Pyramid* because all students are part of Primary Level Prevention and Instruction *always*, even while receiving Secondary or Tertiary Prevention. Secondary and Tertiary Interventions are always in addition to Primary Prevention, never in place of it.

Figure 2.2
Multi-Level Prevention System

Approximately 5%

Approximately 15%

Approximately 80%

Tertiary Prevention:
Specialized
Individualized assessment
Data-informed
Higher intensity, longer duration
    systems for students at high risk

Secondary Prevention:
Specialized group
Assessment, data-informed
Targeted intervention
Systems for students at-risk
Rapid response, high efficiency

Primary Prevention:
Schoolwide core instruction
Feedback for all students in
    academic and behavioral
    expectations
Preventive and proactive
*Students never stop receiving this
    instruction*

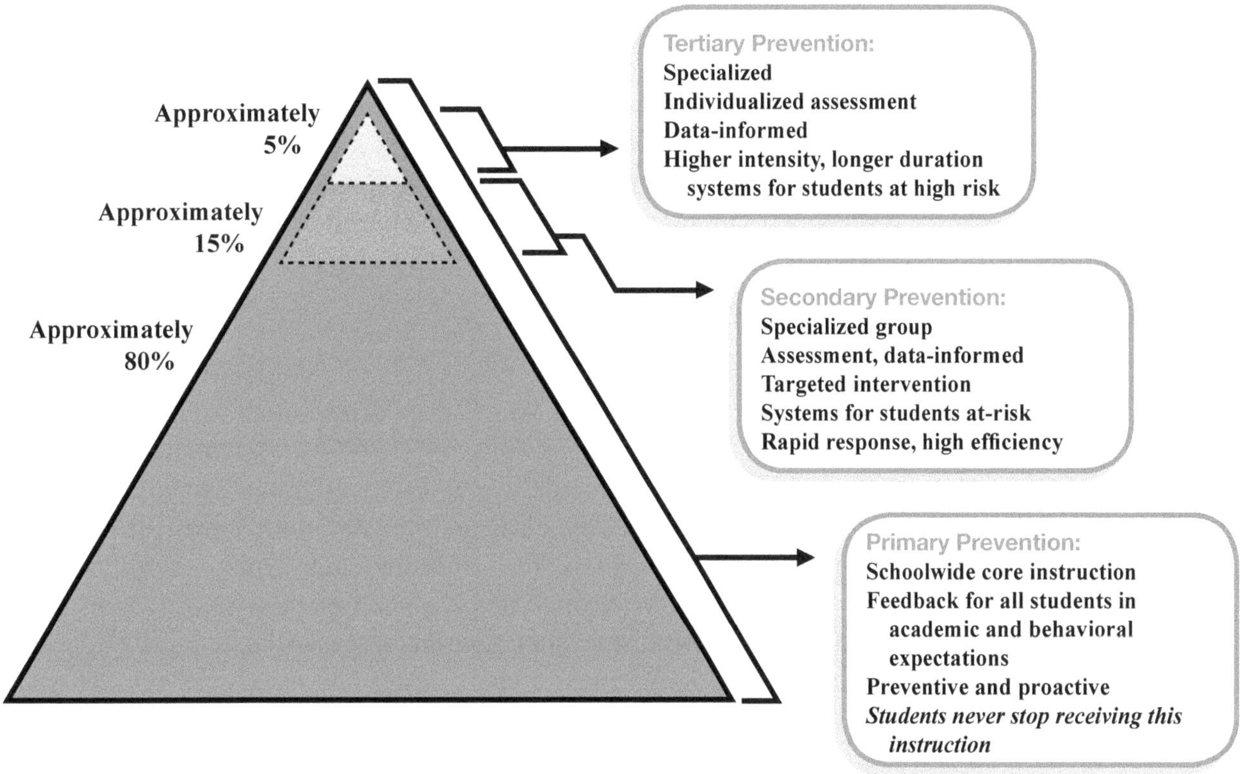

Note: The term *tier* is often used in schools; however, the National Center on Response to Intervention uses the terms *Primary, Secondary,* and *Tertiary Levels* to avoid any misconceptions that students are moved someplace else – such as pulled out of the classroom. The authors support the use of the level terminology.

*When teachers provide well-articulated, standards-based, aligned curriculum that is delivered with evidence-based, differentiated, and targeted instruction to match the characteristics of the learners in a classroom with clear, explicitly taught expectations, procedures and routines, the academic and behavioral needs of approximately 80% of the student population in a school will be met at the **Primary Level**, 100% of the time.*

The theory that underlies the three-level RtI structure is this: When teachers provide well-articulated, standards-based, aligned curriculum that is delivered with evidence-based, differentiated, and targeted instruction to match the characteristics of the learners in a classroom with clear, explicitly taught expectations, procedures and routines, the academic and behavioral needs of approximately 80% of the student population in a school will be met at the *Primary Level,* 100% of the time. Schools that have a large percentage of at-risk students may find they have what is often called an inverted triangle or upside down pyramid. These schools may have 20% or fewer of students who are benefiting from *Primary Level* instruction. For our system to be responsive, teachers must adjust core instruction to advance these at-risk students at least one grade level. A focus on *Primary Level* instruction that supports student learning will be paramount for obtaining the outcomes desired.

*When the **Primary instruction** is effective, 20% or fewer of a school's student population should need **Secondary or Tertiary Level Interventions.***

Once *Primary Level* strategies for academic proficiencies and behavior competencies are in place and delivered with *integrity and fidelity* (i.e., consistently implemented as they are designed) within and among grade levels, staff can identify students for whom this is not enough. When the *Primary* instruction is effective, 20% or fewer of a school's student population should need *Secondary or Tertiary Level Interventions.*

*The **Secondary Intervention Level** builds on Primary Instruction and is mostly delivered in small groups within the general education classroom, by the classroom teacher, with support from resource or instructional specialists for academic areas of concern.*

Students who need *Secondary Level Interventions* are provided with supports targeted to specific areas in which they demonstrate a risk for failure or need for support. The *Secondary Intervention Level* builds on *Primary Instruction* and is mostly delivered in small groups within the general education classroom, by the classroom teacher, with support from resource or instructional specialists for academic areas of concern. *Secondary Interventions* in behavior often involve small group social skills instruction, re-teaching of behavioral expectations, increases in the frequency of behavior monitoring (i.e. daily behavior charts instead of weekly behavior charts), or developing an individual system for monitoring expected behaviors.

For students who demonstrate significant risk of failure on universal screening or students who do not make sufficient progress with instruction and intervention provided at the *Primary* and *Secondary Levels,* a *Tertiary Level of Intervention* is provided that is more intensive, targeted, focused, and powerful. At the *Tertiary Level,* intensive, evidence-based interventions are provided to individual students or to very small groups for academics and behavior, sometimes delivered by a specialist or special education teacher. Additional diagnostic assessments may be conducted for students at this level to further drive instruction and intervention. For students with behavior concerns, this will likely involve a *Functional Behavior Assessment (FBA).* Typically, 5% or fewer of a school's student population require this level of intensive intervention.

When students demonstrate insufficient progress after receiving continued or intensive intervention, the school may consider referral for evaluation of eligibility as a child with a disability.

Core Principles of RtI

While the concept of RtI has been around for some time, the appearance of this phrase in the reauthorization of the Individuals with Disabilities Education Improvement Act (IDEA) in 2004 created a wealth of literature to help schools with shaping and implementing a responsive system. Out of this literature, as well as the experience of the authors, we can identify some core principles for implementation which may enlighten the reader regarding the need for CSI with (if not before) RtI implementation. Essential features of an effective system for RtI involve –

- ◆ Implementing agreed upon universal supports for desired behavior and academic outcomes by providing highly effective and responsive instruction and interventions based on the school's data.

- ◆ Less reliance on teacher nomination alone to trigger a need for intervention.

- ◆ Increasing reliance on data-informed decision making for improved student outcomes.

- ◆ Utilizing screening and progress monitoring assessments to identify students in need of strategic and intensive interventions to address areas of risk.

- ◆ Providing increasingly intense, targeted interventions using evidence-based practices that are matched to identified areas of risk and individual learning needs.

- ◆ Monitoring student performance strategically and throughout the school year to address areas of risk in order to prevent failure.

- ◆ Preventing unnecessary referrals for evaluation of the need for special education services by providing responsive instruction and timely intervention.

At the **Tertiary Level,** intensive, evidence-based interventions are provided to individual students or to very small groups for academics and behavior, sometimes delivered by a specialist or special education teacher.

Typically, 5% or fewer of a school's student population require this level of intensive intervention.

◆ Creating effective collaboration structures and data teams to assist with decision making, monitoring, and evaluating the system.

◆ Monitoring the coherence of the system's implementation of practices in order to continuously improve all levels of instruction and intervention.

◆ Soliciting input, communicating with, and including parents and other external support systems throughout the process.

Intent of RtI

The intent of RtI is to make our systems, our schools, and our classrooms more responsive to the demonstrated instructional needs and individual differences of our students, and to match those demonstrated needs with evidence-based, effective instruction and interventions to *prevent failure.* RtI is not simply a set of interventions; it is a systematic model of preventive and supplementary instructional services for students who are at risk for school failure.

The determination for eligibility and need of special education services too often becomes the focus for development and implementation of systems of RtI. Some staff view RtI as a way to delay special education identification – or as an obstacle to that inevitable outcome. Helping staff understand RtI as a preventive *system* may help this focus move from an inaccurate belief of the way to prevent students from receiving special education services to a much more accurate belief of designing processes and supports to ensure successful performance for *every* student – the way we do business. Helping staff understand the difference between a deficit and a disability may also aid staff in understanding when a special education referral is appropriate. It is important for school staff to understand the nuance of disability and understand in some cases, such as suspected autism, vision impairments, intellectual disabilities, and other developmental disabilities, immediate referral for special education evaluation may be appropriate without any RtI efforts.

Deficit Versus Risk Model

Teachers, administrators, and even community members will need assistance in shifting thinking from our traditional model of identifying learning deficits in students to a model for identifying and addressing risk factors that lead to poor learning outcomes. While these two models share some common features, such as being child centered and data driven, there are key differences worthy of our attention. One key difference involves how assessment is viewed and used. In a *deficit model,* assessments are used to help identify services or supports to decrease the distance between desired

The intent of RtI is to make our systems, our schools, and our classrooms more responsive to the demonstrated instructional needs and individual differences of our students, and to match those demonstrated needs with evidence-based, effective instruction and interventions to prevent failure.

Teachers, administrators, and even community members will need assistance in shifting thinking from our traditional model of identifying learning deficits in students to a model for identifying and addressing risk factors that lead to poor learning outcomes.

and actual performance. Efforts are focused on reducing the deficit; and we count it a fortunate, but rare occasion, when we eliminate a deficit in learning. In a *risk model,* assessments are used to identify patterns of performance and subskills present and absent in order to address these areas of risk and develop skills needed for success. Efforts are focused on building skills and returning the learner to a healthy state for future learning to take hold, with the intent that core instruction and universal supports will be sufficient for continued success. Reducing a *deficit* implies recovering a loss or 'closing the gap' between failure and success. Reducing *risk* implies gaining skills or abilities to prevent the gap from occurring.

*Reducing a **deficit** implies recovering a loss or 'closing the gap' between failure and success. Reducing **risk** implies gaining skills or abilities to prevent the gap from occurring.*

Figure 2.3 shows some of the differences and commonalities between the deficit and risk models.

Figure 2.3
Differences and Similarities:
Deficit and Risk Models

Deficit Model　　　　　　　　**Risk Model**

Similarities

Deficit Model
- Reactive, treatment oriented
- Wait for student to fail
- Remedial approach
- Broad areas of need
- Focuses on "closing the gap"
- Longer intervention time because students are farther behind
- Often done to document need for special education referral
- May lead to retention or needing to repeat a subject due to failure

Similarities
- Addresses student learning needs and helping students be successful
- Reduces problems
- Increases achievement
- Standards-based
- Data-informed instruction
- Small group instruction
- Evidence-based, targeted interventions
- Good intentions

Risk Model
- Proactive, prevention oriented
- Early Intervention
- Growth mindset
- Focus on *all* students and areas of need
- Prevents the gap
- Pre-planning for anticipated needs results in shorter intervention time
- Prevents the need for referral
- May reduce numbers retained or asked to repeat due to failure

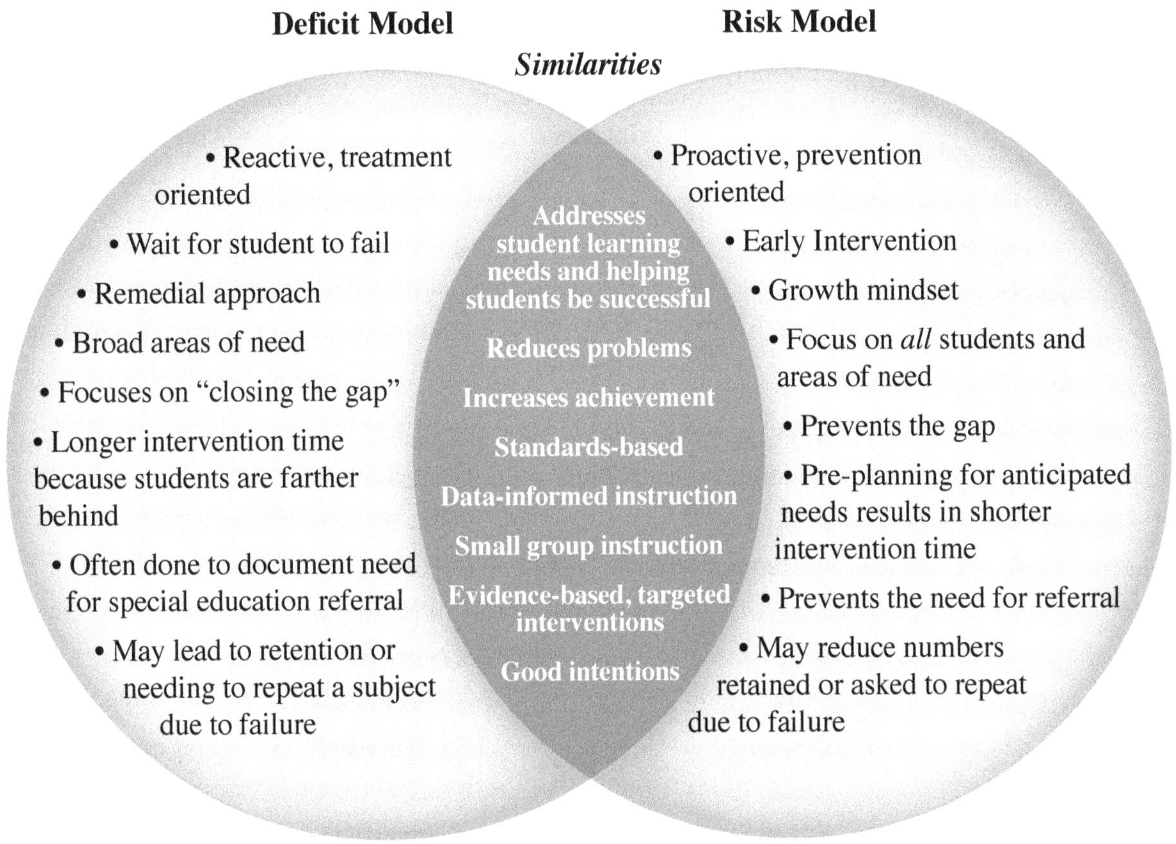

A primary assumption associated with *deficit model* thinking is that when a student is struggling, there must be an inherent factor within the student contributing to failure. Whereas a primary assumption associated with *risk model* thinking is that when a student is struggling, there must be an inherent factor within curriculum delivery contributing to failure. Therefore, when a student is struggling, the curriculum delivery must be adjusted, rather than immediately assuming a disability, poverty, or other student factors are causing failure. When staff provide excuses to explain student performance with statements like, "He is doing the best he can, considering . . .," or persist in providing one-to-one assistance to students, they are most likely engaged in *deficit* thinking using a reactive approach. When staff ask more reflective questions about their own teaching strategies and the effectiveness of classroom structures, they are most likely focused on reducing *risk,* using a proactive approach.

Staff must understand that RtI is a *risk model* – not a *deficit model* – in order to experience the promised outcomes of RtI.

Components of RtI

Many complex issues must be considered when designing and implementing an system of RtI. Which assessments will be used for screening and progress monitoring, level and type of interventions, location and delivery of intervention sessions, frequency and duration of intervention sessions, and the difficulty of teaching multiple interventions are just a few of the logistics to consider. Future chapters, and specifically the *RtI Implementation Guide,* will assist teams in developing a comprehensive system that is strategically designed to address the unique characteristics of your school.

In addition to designing and delivering research-based instruction and interventions at each level, schools must have:

- *Screening and progress monitoring assessments* that are frequent, brief, reliable, valid, accurate predictors of risk and sensitive to small amounts of growth.
- *Universal strategies* that are research-based for achieving academic outcomes and meeting behavioral expectations.
- *Evidence-based interventions* at multiple levels and of varying type, number, length, duration, and intensities.
- *Cut points,* or cut scores, that specify the score on assessments to differentiate students who are at risk for poor learning outcomes from those who are not. These scores may be either criterion referenced or norm referenced.

---

*Staff must understand that RtI is a **risk model** – not a **deficit model** – in order to experience the promised outcomes of RtI.*

*The **RtI Implementation Guide,** will assist teams in developing a comprehensive system that is strategically designed to address the unique characteristics of your school.*

Schools must have:

- *Screening and progress monitoring assessments*
- *Universal strategies*
- *Evidence-based interventions*
- *Cut points*
- *Collaborative processes*
- *Referral process and documentation*

◆ *Collaborative processes* for utilizing data to inform decisions regarding intervention effectiveness and the potential need of referral for consideration of evaluation for special services.

◆ *Referral process and documentation,* although not the primary focus of RtI, are necessary to support the consideration of evaluation for students who do not respond to multiple interventions as expected.

Integrity and Fidelity of Implementation

In a *systemic* RtI model, *integrity and fidelity* are important at both the school level (e.g., implementation of the system) and the teacher level (e.g., implementation of instruction and interventions). Although *integrity and fidelity* of implementation are critical to an intervention's successful outcome, the practical challenges associated with achieving high levels of integrity and fidelity are well documented. Factors that reduce *integrity and fidelity* of implementation include the following:

◆ *Complexity.* The more complex the intervention, the lower the fidelity because of the level of implementation difficulty. (This factor includes time needed for instruction in the intervention.)

◆ *Materials and resources required.* If new or substantial resources are required, they need to be readily accessible and accompanied by adequate training and professional learning for implementation fidelity.

◆ *Perceived and actual effectiveness (credibility).* Even with a solid research base, if teachers believe the approach will not be effective, or if it is inconsistent with their teaching style, they will not implement it well.

◆ *Interventionists.* The number, expertise, and motivation of individuals who deliver the intervention are factors in the level of fidelity of implementation.

(Johnson, Mellard, Fuchs, & McKnight, 2006)

Development of the RtI Implementation Guide through the chapters that follow will allow schools to identify and address issues associated with *integrity and fidelity* as they plan.

Implementation with integrity is putting a plan, process, or program into effect with accuracy and consistency.

Implementation with fidelity is carrying out that plan, process, or program the way it is intended to be implemented.

Factors that reduce integrity and fidelity of implementation include the following:

◆ *Complexity.*

◆ *Materials and resources required.*

◆ *Perceived and actual effectiveness (credibility).*

◆ *Interventionists.*

Relationship of RtI to Special Education

RtI provides an alternative or additional means of gathering information to be used when identifying students in need of special education evaluation, but this is not the intent, purpose, or focus of the system of RtI.

The RtI model acts as a safeguard, ensuring that a student is not given a label for a disability inappropriately.

RtI provides an alternative or additional means of gathering information to be used when identifying students in need of special education evaluation, but this is not the intent, purpose, or focus of the system of RtI. When a student is identified as "at risk" in school, a team provides interventions of increasing intensity to help the student develop skills similar to the rest of her/his peers. After multiple interventions have been tried and proven ineffective, the student may then be referred for consideration of special education evaluation. Opponents of RtI say this is a way to allow some school districts to avoid or delay identifying students as needing special education services. Proponents of RtI assert, based on research, that RtI is a way to ensure each student is afforded the opportunity to learn and be proficient. When interventions work, fewer students, particularly those in minority populations, are referred for special education, and equity emerges in the special education referral process. The RtI model acts as a safeguard, ensuring that a student is not given a label for a disability inappropriately.

The effort behind designing, implementing, monitoring, and evaluating a system of RtI that will lead to promised outcomes is not easy to initiate and sustain. While educators in schools that experience promised outcomes report they would not go back to the way they did things before RtI, many readily admit they are working harder (and smarter) than before.

Book Study Questions

1. What are the essential principles of a system for responsiveness to interventions?

2. What is the intent of RtI?

3. What are the components of RtI?

4. How do the components of RtI ensure the intent of RtI is fulfilled?

Application Opportunities

1. What is the intent of your school's system of RtI? If a system of RtI is not in place, what essential features, attitudes, or beliefs held by your staff are supportive of implementing such a system?

2. What are some common misperceptions about RtI at your school? Who holds these misperceptions or beliefs? How can you clarify the intent of RtI?

3. Which components or features of RtI are working in your school? Which are not? Do you know what needs to be done to improve or establish these components?

CHAPTER 3

Continuous School Improvement: Study and Commit

Continuously improving schools clarify whom they have as students, understand where the learning organization is right now on all measures, consider processes, as well as results, create visions that will make a difference for whom they have as students, help everyone get on the same page with understanding how to achieve a vision, and know if what the learning organization is doing is making a difference.

Victoria L. Bernhardt

When staff design systems of RtI consistent with continuous school improvement, they begin with –

- a comprehensive review of all their data to answer the question, *Where are we now?*

- a study of contributing causes of undesirable results and deeper data analysis to answer the question, *How did we get to where we are now?*

- the creation of a shared vision to answer the question, *Where do we want to be?*

- the development of structures required to get all staff implementing the vision to answer the question, *How are we going to get to where we want to be?* and

- a formative and summative evaluation structure in place to answer the question, *Is what we are doing making a difference?*

By answering these key questions, staff agree on beliefs about student learning. They learn how to improve student learning in every grade level, in every subject area, and with every student group, and then how to create a continuum of learning that makes sense for students. By doing this work, staff is set up to redesign the school day, if necessary, in order to establish a schoolwide prevention system. By doing this work, these staff complete a comprehensive needs assessment and set themselves up for comprehensive evaluation.

Continuous School Improvement Framework

Figure 3.1 displays a framework for continuous school improvement that helps schools design, implement, monitor, and evaluate their system of RtI. As the figure shows, for a school to create a learning organization that will make a difference for all students and all teachers, staff must answer five essential and logical questions.

- Where are we now?
- How did we get to where we are?
- Where do we want to be?
- How are we going to get to where we want to be?
- Is what we are doing making a difference?

These questions are detailed on the pages that follow the figure, along with why it is important to consider the questions and their answers.

Figure 3.1
Continuous School Improvement Framework

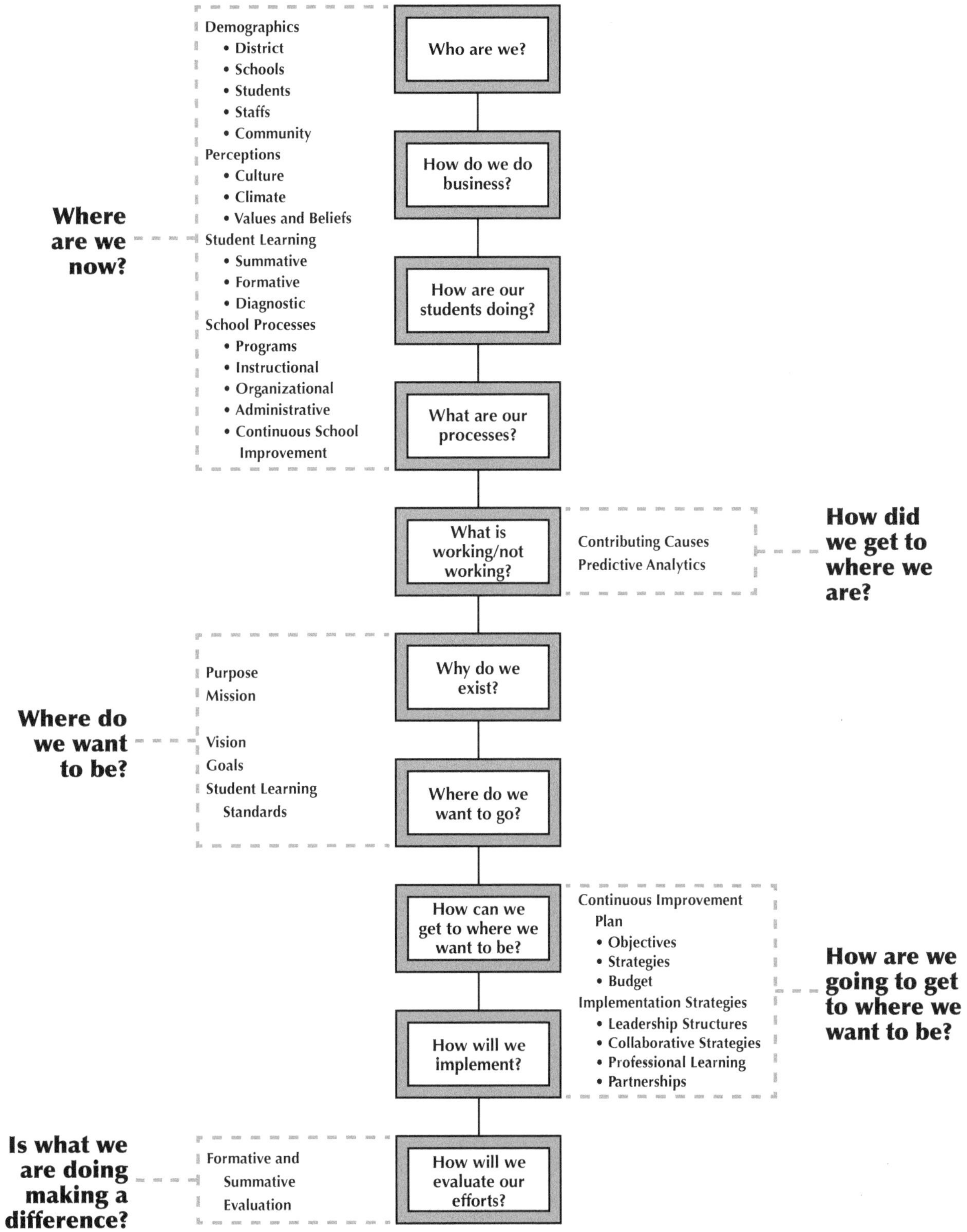

Where are we now?

Demographics
- District
- Schools
- Students
- Staffs
- Community

Perceptions
- Culture
- Climate
- Values and Beliefs

Student Learning
- Summative
- Formative
- Diagnostic

School Processes
- Programs
- Instructional
- Organizational
- Administrative
- Continuous School Improvement

Who are we?

How do we do business?

How are our students doing?

What are our processes?

What is working/not working?

How did we get to where we are?

Contributing Causes
Predictive Analytics

Where do we want to be?

Purpose
Mission

Vision
Goals
Student Learning Standards

Why do we exist?

Where do we want to go?

How can we get to where we want to be?

How will we implement?

How are we going to get to where we want to be?

Continuous Improvement Plan
- Objectives
- Strategies
- Budget

Implementation Strategies
- Leadership Structures
- Collaborative Strategies
- Professional Learning
- Partnerships

Is what we are doing making a difference?

Formative and Summative Evaluation

How will we evaluate our efforts?

Data Analysis for Continuous School Improvement (3rd ed.), (p. 14). By V.L. Bernhardt, 2013, New York, NY: Routledge.

Where Are We Now?

Knowing where a school is now is the part of planning for continuous school improvement that requires a comprehensive and honest look at all the school's data – not just student learning results. Figure 3.2 shows the categories of data that are used to answer four sub-questions of Where are we now?

- *Who are we?* answered through demographic data.
- *How do we do business?* mostly answered through perceptions and organizational assessments.
- *How are our students doing?* answered through formative and summative student learning results.
- *What are our processes?* answered through listing and analyzing existing programs and processes.

Relationship of CSI to RtI

Multiple measures of data help us accurately identify students who are at risk for poor learning outcomes. With the support of this comprehensive data analysis, schools can develop an effective schoolwide prevention system that addresses the needs of all students. By looking at all measures honestly, schools can identify common learning profiles and needs of students as well as research programs and processes that will enhance outcomes based on that profile. This comprehensive schoolwide data analysis is paramount for schools with upside down pyramids or large numbers of students at risk for poor learning outcomes as it will help teachers learn what types of strategies and learning opportunities match learning needs of students in our system. As a result, 80% or more of our general student population will be able to achieve expected levels of performance through Primary Prevention, recognizing that our Primary Prevention may include instructional approaches that are used at the Secondary or Tertiary Levels in other systems.

Comprehensive schoolwide data analysis also allows us to identify targeted, specific strategies and processes to support students in need of Secondary and Tertiary Prevention in our system. Using comprehensive schoolwide data analysis to develop and continuously inform RtI processes will reduce the inequity that comes with relying on each teacher to determine when to provide interventions or when to request additional assistance.

Knowing where a school is now is the part of planning for continuous school improvement that requires a comprehensive and honest look at all the school's data – not just student learning results.

Multiple measures of data help us accurately identify students who are at risk for poor learning outcomes. With the support of this comprehensive data analysis, schools can develop an effective schoolwide prevention system that addresses the needs of all students.

Using comprehensive schoolwide data analysis to develop and continuously inform RtI processes will reduce the inequity that comes with relying on each teacher to determine when to provide interventions or when to request additional assistance.

Figure 3.2
Multiple Measures of Data

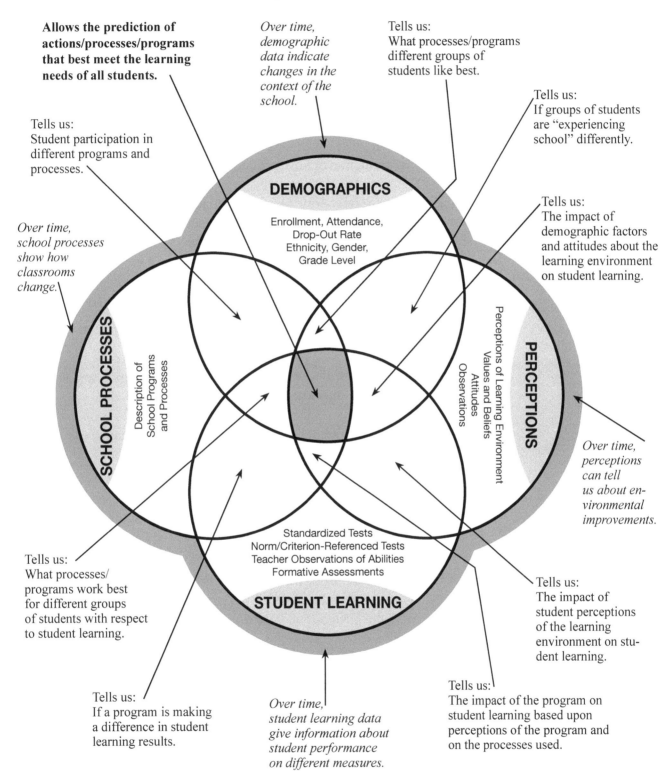

Allows the prediction of actions/processes/programs that best meet the learning needs of all students.

Over time, demographic data indicate changes in the context of the school.

Tells us: What processes/programs different groups of students like best.

Tells us: Student participation in different programs and processes.

Tells us: If groups of students are "experiencing school" differently.

Over time, school processes show how classrooms change.

Tells us: The impact of demographic factors and attitudes about the learning environment on student learning.

DEMOGRAPHICS

Enrollment, Attendance, Drop-Out Rate Ethnicity, Gender, Grade Level

SCHOOL PROCESSES

Description of School Programs and Processes

Perceptions of Learning Environment Values and Beliefs Attitudes Observations

PERCEPTIONS

Over time, perceptions can tell us about environmental improvements.

Standardized Tests
Norm/Criterion-Referenced Tests
Teacher Observations of Abilities
Formative Assessments

STUDENT LEARNING

Tells us: What processes/programs work best for different groups of students with respect to student learning.

Tells us: The impact of student perceptions of the learning environment on student learning.

Tells us: If a program is making a difference in student learning results.

Over time, student learning data give information about student performance on different measures.

Tells us: The impact of the program on student learning based upon perceptions of the program and on the processes used.

Data Analysis for Continuous School Improvement (3rd ed.), (p. 17). By V.L. Bernhardt, 2013, New York, NY: Routledge.

Who Are We?

Demographic data are important because they provide the context of the school, and answer the continuous school improvement question, *Who are we?* Demographic data include enrollment in the school, by grade level, gender, ethnicity/race, language proficiency, indicators of poverty, etc. Demographic data also include attendance, behavior (e.g., office referrals, suspensions, expulsions), retentions, drop-out/graduation rates, students identified for special needs/exceptionalities, program enrollment, and staff demographics. Three years of demographic data can show a trend. Five years will give an even better idea of how your data are changing, and will assist with the prediction of how your population might change in the future.

Demographic data show how the student population has changed over time and will continue to change, which can give staff an idea of what strategies they need to study and learn to better meet the needs of the students they have now and are projected to have in the future. Demographic data also show the leadership philosophy of the school, through indicators of which and how students are disciplined, referred for special education placement, advanced placement, gifted programs, etc.

Schools who answer the question *Who are we?* before beginning RtI do a much better job of designing instructional strategies and targeted interventions because they know the students they serve.

Questions to answer with longitudinal demographic data to help with continuous school improvement and RtI include:

- How has our student population changed over time? How will our population change in the near future? Do we, as staff, have the professional learning, instructional methodologies, and materials in place to teach whom we have as students now and in the future?

- Do we know the who, what, when, where, and why of our behavior and attendance data? What do we need to do differently to ensure the behavior and attendance we want to see with our students?

- Does enrollment in each of the programs we offer represent the overall enrollment of the school? (For example, does the percentage of students, by gender and ethnicity, assigned to gifted classes or special education, correspond to the overall percentage of students, by gender and ethnicity, in the school?) If not, why not, and what do we need to do differently?

Demographic data are important because they provide the context of the school, and answer the continuous school improvement question, Who are we?

*Schools who answer the question **Who are we?** before beginning RtI do a much better job of designing instructional strategies and targeted interventions because they know the students they serve.*

How Do We Do Business?

Perceptions data are important because they can tell us what students, staff, and parents are thinking about the learning organization, and answer the continuous school improvement question, *How do we do business?* The question is answered through assessing the school's culture, climate, and organizational processes. Staff values and beliefs, most often assessed through questionnaires and/or determined during visioning processes, tell a staff if team building or specific professional learning is necessary, and what is possible to implement. Perceptions can also show where the deep changes are happening in the school with respect to staff values and beliefs.

Student and parent questionnaires can add different perspectives to the information generated from staff data. Students can report what it takes for them to learn and how they are being taught and treated. Parent perceptions can help staff know what supports are needed for parents to become more involved in their child's learning. Parental involvement maybe a "new" concept for immigrant and refugees. They might need additional support.

A schoolwide self-assessment can provide an overview of where the staff believes the school is on the measures that make a difference for school improvement or RtI implementation. These assessments often surprise administrators who may think all staff members are thinking about school in the same way. If a school staff does not know how it does business, in reality, it could be creating plans and structures that might never be implemented or might not lead to the desired outcomes.

Questions to answer with perceptions data that will assist with continuous school improvement and RtI include:

- How does our student population perceive the learning environment? Do they feel like they belong, that they are safe, that they are cared for, that they have fun learning? Do they feel challenged by the work they are being asked to do?

- How do parents perceive the learning environment? Do they feel welcome in the school? Do they know how to help their children learn at home? Do they feel the school is a good school and that it has a good public image?

- How do staff perceive the learning environment? Do staff members feel it is challenging, safe, and welcoming to students, staff, and parents? Do staff members feel there is a shared vision in place, that everyone knows what her/his job is in the school, and that staff collaborate to make learning consistent across grade levels? Do staff believe what they are asked to do will lead to student learning growth? Do staff believe that all students can

*Perceptions data are important because they can tell us what students, staff, and parents are thinking about the learning organization, and answer the continuous school improvement question, **How do we do business?***

If a school staff does not know how it does business, in reality, it could be creating plans and structures that might never be implemented or might not lead to the desired outcomes.

learn? Do teaching strategies reflect the staff belief that every student can learn?

How Are Our Students Doing?

Student learning data show if schools are meeting the needs of all students and uncover strengths and areas for improvement to answer the continuous school improvement question How are our students doing? *Answering the question requires a synthesis of student learning data in all subject areas, disaggregated by all student groups, by grade levels, by following the same groups of students (cohorts) over time, as well as looking at individual student learning growth. If students are not proficient, teachers need to know what the students know and what they do not know. If students are not proficient, teachers also need to know how many, and by how much, students must improve. Looking at student learning across grade levels also reveals if a school has instructional coherence. *Instructional coherence* is the alignment and consistent delivery of curriculum, instruction, and assessments by grade level as well as across grade levels. It is about creating a continuum of learning that makes sense for *every* student.

Student learning data include diagnostic assessments, classroom assessments, formative assessments, state/provincial assessments, and grades. In a perfect scenario, we would be clear and agree on what we want students to know and be able to do by the end of the year, course, or lesson. We would use formative assessments to discover what students know and do not know as we begin to plan instruction for the students. We would then assess on a regular basis to understand what students are learning and which students need extra support, and adjust instruction to meet student needs. Then we would assess to know if the students learned what we wanted them to learn. If some students have not learned what we wanted them to learn, plans are put in place for appropriate instruction and intervention.

Questions to answer with student learning data to assist with continuous school improvement and RtI include:

- ◆ Are teachers teaching to the standards?
- ◆ Is student learning increasing over time, for the school, by grade level and subject area, and for each student?
- ◆ In which subject areas are students strongest, and in which subject areas do they need more support?
- ◆ Is there instructional coherence? Does each grade level build on previous grade levels and prepare students for the future?

Student learning data show if schools are meeting the needs of all students and uncover strengths and areas for improvement to answer the continuous school improvement question **How are our students doing?**

Instructional coherence is the alignment and consistent delivery of curriculum, instruction, and assessments by grade level as well as across grade levels. It is about creating a continuum of learning that makes sense for **every** *student.*

Staff who answer the question **How are our students doing?** *before beginning RtI know what students know and do not know and are able to establish Primary Prevention to meet the needs of at least 80% of their students, as well as design quality Secondary and Tertiary Interventions that will meet the needs of every student.*

Staff who answer the question *How are our students doing?* before beginning RtI know what students know and do not know and are able to establish Primary Prevention to meet the needs of at least 80% of their students, as well as design quality Secondary and Tertiary Interventions that will meet the needs of every student.

What Are Our Processes?

School process data are important because they tell us about the way we work, about how we get the results we are getting, set us up to know what is working and what is not working, and answer the continuous school improvement question, *What are our processes?*

School processes include curriculum, instruction and assessment strategies, discipline approaches, leadership, and programs. These are the elements of our organizations over which we have almost complete control, but we tend to measure these elements the least. Answering this question calls for a complete accounting and evaluation of all programs and processes operating throughout the learning organization.

Questions to answer with school process data to assist with continuous school improvement and RtI include:

- ◆ What is the intent of each program that we operate? Whom is each program intending to serve, and whom is it serving?

- ◆ How will we know if each program is successful? What are the results?

- ◆ To what degree are the programs being implemented?

Staff who answer *What are our processes?* before beginning RtI know what programs and processes have been implemented to help every student. They understand what is working and what is not working; what to keep and what to revise. Staff also know how many and how students are referred for special education evaluation as well as who and how many are eligible.

Looking Across the Multiple Measures of Data

Figure 3.2 shows the categories of data that are important to gather and analyze in schools for continuous school improvement. The graphic also indicates that intersecting these types of data will answer deeper questions. Looking across all types of data is important for seeing the linkages in the data results. There might be issues that show up in demographics, perceptions, and school processes that can help explain how a school is getting the results it is getting in student learning, that could be an easy fix. Looking across all data can help improve all content areas at the same time.

*Staff who answer **What are our processes?** before beginning RtI know what programs and processes have been implemented to help every student. They understand what is working and what is not working; what to keep and what to revise. Staff also know how many and how students are referred for special education evaluation as well as who and how many are eligible.*

Looking across all types of data is important for seeing the linkages in the data results.

Gaps are determined by synthesizing the differences between the results the school is getting with its current processes and the results the school wants to get.

Contributing cause analyses, along with comprehensive data analysis, help schools understand how they are getting their current results, and what it will take to eliminate the gaps.

How Did We Get to Where We Are?

Gaps are determined by synthesizing the differences between the results the school is getting with its current processes and the results the school wants to get. Contributing cause analyses, along with comprehensive data analysis, help schools understand how they are getting their current results, and what it will take to eliminate the gaps.

It is particularly important to know how the school is getting its current results in all areas of student learning, so processes that are achieving the school's desired results are repeated, and strategies and structures that are not making a difference are eliminated.

Many schools begin and end their school improvement plans by looking at the gaps between where they are now and where they want to be, with respect to student learning results only. While these data provide valuable information, looking only at the gaps does not give schools a complete picture. By starting and ending with the gaps, schools miss the opportunities to improve, innovate, and rethink their systems.

Staff who begin RtI by answering How did we get to where we are? understand how they are getting the results they are getting now, and what needs to change to get different results. These staff members can also identify obstacles that could get in the way of implementing RtI with integrity and fidelity, unless certain adjustments are made.

Where Do We Want to Be?

A school defines its destination through its mission, vision, goals, and objectives – aligned with the district's mission, vision, goals, and standards (i.e., student grade level expectations), which, in turn, are aligned with the state mission, vision, goals, and standards. The school's mission and vision must reflect the core values and beliefs of the staff, merged from personal values and beliefs. Creating a vision from core values and beliefs ensures a vision to which all staff members can commit. Without a vision to which all staff members commit, a school's collective efforts have no target.

Figure 3.3 shows that *Random Acts of Improvement* result when there is no specific target. Strong leadership inspires a shared vision and ensures its implementation. A strong leader also encourages and models the analysis and use of data. A continuous school improvement process ensures that all professional learning is focused on implementing the vision, that all staff members understand their roles in implementing the vision and helping students learn, and that there is evaluation to know how to improve on an ongoing basis to reach school goals. A vision which is shared and to which all staff are committed is the key to getting *Focused Acts of Improvement* (Figure 3.4).

Staff who begin RtI by answering How did we get to where we are? understand how they are getting the results they are getting now, and what needs to change to get different results.

Creating a vision from core values and beliefs ensures a vision to which all staff members can commit. Without a vision to which all staff members commit, a school's collective efforts have no target.

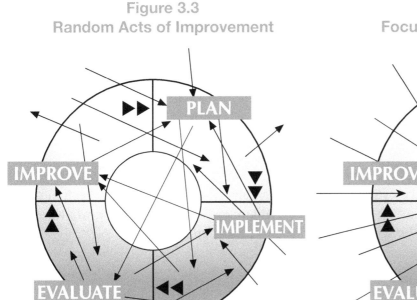

Figure 3.3
Random Acts of Improvement

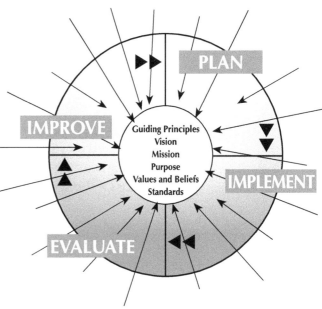

Figure 3.4
Focused Acts of Improvement

Staff who answer the question *Where do we want to be?* before beginning the design of RtI get staff commitments to a mission and vision reflecting core values and beliefs, as well as commitments to what curricula they will implement, how they will instruct and assess, and the environment they believe will assist them in ensuring that *every* student will learn.

How Are We Going to Get to Where We Want to Be?

Key to unlocking how the vision will be implemented and how gaps will be eliminated is answering the continuous school improvement question, *How are we going to get to where we want to be?* An action plan, consisting of goals, objectives, strategies, activities, measurement of strategies and activities, person(s) responsible, due dates, timelines, and required resources, needs to be developed to implement and achieve the vision and to eliminate the contributing causes of the gaps.

Leadership structures, professional learning, structured collaboration to utilize data, shared professional learning experiences, and parent/community involvement and partnerships are key elements for ensuring implementation of the shared vision. Action plans must include how and when decisions will be made, identify professional learning and collaboration required to gain new skills and knowledge, and clarify how working with partners will help with achieving the vision.

Staff who answer the question **Where do we want to be?** before beginning the design of RtI get staff commitments to a mission and vision reflecting core values and beliefs, as well as commitments to what curricula they will implement, how they will instruct and assess, and the environment they believe will assist them in ensuring that every student will learn.

Key to unlocking how the vision will be implemented and how gaps will be eliminated is answering the continuous school improvement question, How are we going to get to where we want to be?

*Staff who answer the question **How are we going to get to where we want to be?** before starting RtI are able to design a system of RtI that compliments existing efforts and desired outcomes. They are also able to build on leadership and staff collaboration structures to ensure success.*

*Staff who answer the question **Is What We Are Doing Making a Difference?** before starting RtI are able to develop a monitoring and evaluation system that will ensure that RtI will be implemented with integrity and fidelity, and that the efforts will result in desired outcomes.*

Staff who answer the question *How are we going to get to where we want to be?* before starting RtI are able to design a system of RtI that compliments existing efforts and desired outcomes. They are also able to build on leadership and staff collaboration structures to ensure success.

Is What We Are Doing Making a Difference?

Formative evaluation and reflective learning are required to assess the effectiveness of all school programs and processes, the alignment of all parts of the system to the vision, and to determine the answer to the continuous school improvement question, *Is What We Are Doing Making a Difference?* Summative evaluations, i.e., at the end of the year, allow reflection on all the parts of the system, and the alignment of the parts to the whole, and to assess if the school made the expected difference.

Evaluation must be both formative – as it looks at the success of the various parts of the plan – and summative, as it looks at the plan as a whole and at the end of each phase.

Staff who answer the question *Is What We Are Doing Making a Difference?* before starting RtI are able to develop a monitoring and evaluation system that will ensure that RtI will be implemented with *integrity and fidelity,* and that the efforts will result in desired outcomes.

Book Study Questions

Consider Figure 3.1, the Continuous School Improvement Framework:

1. Why is it important to implement continuous school improvement before designing a system of RtI?

2. Why is a comprehensive needs assessment important to complete before creating a vision or a system of RtI?

3. Why is it important to know how a school is getting its results before designing a system of RtI?

Application Opportunities

Before designing your system of RtI, it would be good to do the following:

1. Review your multiple measures of data and create a comprehensive needs assessment to understand what is working and what is not working, and to know which students are not growing academically each year.

2. Create a shared vision to get staff commitments to curriculum, instruction, assessment, and the learning environment.

3. Establish a system of monitoring and evaluation.

CHAPTER 4

Planning with the RtI Implementation Guide

Research has shown that if people do not have clear processes and procedures, they are unlikely to achieve desired outcomes.

National Center on Response to Intervention

After *Studying and Committing* to RtI, staff must begin the strenuous but exciting journey of planning for the design and implementation of their system of RtI. With the details clearly thought out before implementation, staff's transparent understanding of the entire system makes it more likely all aspects of RtI will be implemented with integrity and fidelity. With the details clearly written, it is easier for the planners to determine how the components will work together, to monitor and later evaluate what is working and what is not to guide revisions.

Many school Leadership Teams, who leave RtI workshops eager to implement RtI, return to school to find hesitation and low confidence to implement on the part of staff. The authors designed the RtI Implementation Guide to enable teams to document all aspects of the system of RtI, to implement, monitor, and evaluate, with *integrity and fidelity.* The Implementation Guide will help RtI Teams get their system of RtI off the ground – the right way – from the beginning. The Guide appears in total on the accompanying website, www.routledge.com/cw/bernhardtandhebert, and is used in the discussions of RtI components in the chapters that follow. Many tools in the RtI Implementation Guide include summaries of the purpose of the component, taken from literature, on the first page followed by guiding questions set up in a table on the second page. Some tools are one page examples. These guides are summarized from the literature and the authors' experiences to assist with the design of your school's RtI components and system, as shown in Figure 4.1. In using these tools, change the words to reflect your school.

With the details clearly thought out before implementation, staff's transparent understanding of the entire system makes it more likely all aspects of RtI will be implemented with integrity and fidelity.

*The **Implementation Guide** will help RtI Teams get their system of RtI off the ground – the right way – from the beginning. www.routledge.com/cw/bernhardtandhebert*

Figure 4.1
How to Use the Tools in the RtI Implementation Guide

OUR SCHOOL UNIVERSAL SCREENERS

Universal screening is conducted to identify or predict students who may be at risk for poor learning outcomes.

1 Purpose Taken from literature regarding implementing systems of RtI, use this summary page to share the purpose of each RtI component.

Universal Screeners are:

- Frequent, brief, valid, reliable, accurate predictors of risk, and sensitive to small amounts of growth.
- Measures of essential skills for accessing curriculum and instruction (i.e., read, write, compute).
- Aligned with the curriculum/what you want students to know and be able to do.
- Administered to *all* students, followed by additional testing or short-term Progress Monitoring, for some, to corroborate students' risk status.
- Administered 3 times a year.
- Usually 5 to 30 minutes long.
- Implemented with fidelity.
- Used to identify students at or above cut point (National or Local grade level) who will continue to receive Primary Prevention.
- Used to identify students below cut point – consider Secondary Prevention, along with Primary Prevention.
- Used to identify students significantly below cut point – consider Tertiary Prevention, along with Primary Prevention.

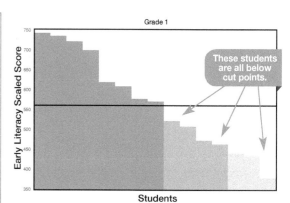

Determining cut scores:
Begin with testing recommendations. Adjust the cut scores, schoolwide, by taking into consideration prior performance and interventions, teacher observations, and support your school has to cover the interventions.

2 Design These are the important questions designers must answer to meet the purpose of the RtI component.

4 Monitor These questions and answers serve to support the monitoring of the implementation of the RtI component. Is what is supposed to be implemented being implemented?

3 Implement These statements represent the way the RtI component is planned to be implemented.

5 Evaluate These questions and answers serve as part of the evaluation of the RtI component. To what degree is staff implementing the components as designed and intended, and how effective is the implementation?

OUR SCHOOL
UNIVERSAL SCREENERS

Components	What tool(s)?	How many times a year is it administered? When is it administered?	Who administers it?	How is it administered? To whom is it administered?	Who scores the tests?	Who interprets the results?	How are the results shared with Teachers? Students? Parents?	What are the cut points? How are cut points identified?	Additional sources to confirm student risk status?	How will you know this tool will accurately classify students?
Reading	• Universal Screener Name	Three times a year: • Beginning of the school year; • Middle of the school year; • End of the school year	• All classroom teachers.	• Laptops in classroom. • All students.	• Computer-based.	• RtI Team initially to get a systemic view of the scores. • RtI team with classroom teachers.	• RtI Team and individual classroom teachers, then schoolwide.	• To be determined by RtI Team, in conjunction with classroom teachers, and screener recommended cut points.	• Classroom performance, previous years' performance and interventions, CBM Diagnostics, and Progress Monitoring probes.	• Review the end of year results, teacher input, and previous year's scores.

Recommendations for Improvement:
Teachers need to learn how to analyze data to understand student needs, and then target their instruction on these needs.

Planning with the RtI Implementation Guide

In this book and the website's Table of Contents, you will see many tools that will help your RtI Team plan for implementation. The tools are referred to as RtI Implementation Guide #, with the # referring to the order in which it appears on the website. Each tool will be described in this chapter along with how to use it in planning. Several tools will be discussed in subsequent chapters as they are used in other stages of implementation.

RtI Implementation Guide #1 is the *Response to Intervention (RtI) Implementation Guide Table of Contents* for the overall RtI Implementation Guide. RtI Teams may adjust the order, before they share with staff, to support the school's planning needs. Insert the name of your school and the names of the RtI Team members on the cover sheet.

RtI Implementation Guide #2, *Implementing a System of Response to Intervention to Improve Learning for Every Student,* is a document that spells out the definition of RtI, its purpose and intent, the components of RtI, and describes the Stages of RtI Implementation. The purpose of this document is to provide a summary for all staff to understand these important points – in the same way.

Our School's System of Response to Intervention document, RtI Implementation Guides #3 and #4, are tools to help staff understand the big picture of RtI for your school. This is a tool every staff member needs to have when completed. RtI Implementation Guide #3 is an elementary school example, although it can be adapted for middle school and high school. RtI Implementation Guide #4 is a secondary example. These guides begin with summaries of the school's Needs Assessments, which help staff understand why RtI is important for reaching every student, and for creating a sense of urgency to implement. The next two columns, *What is the Purpose of RtI?* and *What are the Desired Outcomes for RtI?,* are very important questions that every staff member must know and understand to implement RtI with integrity and fidelity. If the purpose of RtI is not clear and shared, you will have as many ideas about purpose as you have staff members, and RtI can never be implemented as intended. Think big about the outcomes as you plan, or staff will only think about student achievement increases and miss the opportunity to improve student motivation, social competence, behavior, attendance, and building a sense of community in their classrooms. If you are implementing RtI as intended, instruction will improve, climate will be enhanced, students will feel challenged in the work they do, their needs will be met, they will love coming to school, feel like they belong, and every student will show learning growth in both academics and social development. RtI can also be considered *Response to Instruction.* This distinction can guide decisions as you study your core instruction and

RtI Implementation Guide #1 is the Response to Intervention (RtI) Implementation Guide Table of Contents for the overall RtI Implementation Guide.

RtI Implementation Guide #2, Implementing a System of Response to Intervention to Improve Learning for Every Student, is a document that spells out the definition of RtI, its purpose and intent, the components of RtI, and describes the Stages of RtI Implementation.

RtI Implementation Guide #3 is an elementary school example, although it can be adapted for middle school and high school. These tools summarize the System of RtI in your school.

RtI Implementation Guide #4 is a secondary example.

teachers develop a love for learning in students to facilitate learning growth and development. As you create your system of RtI, you want to make sure your *purpose* and *outcomes* are large enough to eliminate the undesirable results that are shown in the needs assessment.

RtI Implementation Guides #3 and #4 provide a column to list *Who Leads RtI?, Who is on the RtI Team?,* and the *Purpose of the RtI Team.* Note your RtI Coordinator and RtI Team. These topics are discussed in greater detail in the section on Roles and Responsibilities.

RtI Implementation Guide #3 and #4 ask *What will RtI Look Like When Fully Implemented?, How Is Implementation Being Monitored?, How Should Implementation be Monitored?, To What Degree is RtI Being Implemented with Integrity and Fidelity?* Just like purpose, if we are not clear on these details, staff will create their own ideas about implementation and monitoring. Once we describe in detail what RtI will look like when fully implemented, we recommend creating a flowchart to show, visually, how to implement RtI. The implementation column and flowchart are invaluable to the monitoring process, as well.

Figure 4.2 shows a partial view of the elementary example shown in Our School's System of Response to Intervention, RtI Implementation Guide #3. Use this tool to create and display your RtI system.

RtI Implementation Guide #5, *Our School Prevention System Flowchart,* presents a comprehensive look of RtI at the Big Picture level. The RtI Team needs to be able to create and monitor implementation through this flowchart. The symbols in yellow are system-level items. Many staff members say, "This is great, but it is not about ME." They want to see a flowchart that focuses on them. RtI Implementation Guide #6, *Prevention System Flowchart: Classroom or Individual Student,* shows the RtI Implementation Guide #5 system level flowchart without those yellow systems symbols to better reflect what is expected of the classroom teacher. RtI Implementation Guide #7, *Planning for RtI at the Secondary Level,* shows a secondary school's planning for RtI, using a flowchart.

RtI Implementation Guide #5, Our School Prevention System Flowchart, presents a comprehensive look of RtI at the Big Picture level.

RtI Implementation Guide #6, Prevention System Flowchart: Classroom or Individual Student, shows the RtI Implementation Guide #5 system level flowchart without those yellow systems symbols to better reflect what is expected of the classroom teacher.

RtI Implementation Guide #7, Planning for RtI at the Secondary Level, shows a secondary school's planning for RtI, using a flowchart.

Figure 4.2
Our School's System of Response to Intervention

NEEDS	PURPOSE OF RtI	LEADS		IMPLEMENTATION		EVALUATION	
What Are Your Needs Assessment Results?	*What Is the Purpose of RtI?*	*What Are the Desired Outcomes for RtI?*	*Who Leads RtI?*	*What Will RtI Look Like When Fully Implemented with Integrity and Fidelity?*	*How Is RtI Implementation Being Monitored?*	*How Will Results Be Measured?*	*What Are the Results?*
Our schoolwide needs assessment results indicate that not all students are showing growth each year. There is a sizeable gap (70%) between our highest performing and lowest performing students. Three student groups specifically need to become more proficient, and show more than one year's growth: • English learners (12% proficient ELA; 17% proficient in Math • Low income (22% proficient in ELA; 20 proficient in Math) • Special education (22% proficient in ELA; 17% proficient in Math) Additionally, our highest performing students are not showing a year's growth. Attendance needs to improve throughout the school (93.5%).	The purpose of RtI at Our School is to: • Implement, in every classroom, quality, research-based instruction and assessment strategies that address students' needs and differences, and are based on the state standards. • Ensure learning growth for all students. • Reduce behavior problems. • Increase student engagement and achievement. • Ensure that all students are primarily educated in the general education	When RtI is implemented as intended: • Instructional coherence and a continuum of learning that makes sense for all students will be evident. • What students learn in one grade level will build on what they learned in previous grade levels, and prepare them for the next grade level. • Individual student achievement results will improve each year. • All students will be proficient in all areas. • No student will need to be retained. • Progress monitoring and common formative assessments conducted within the classroom setting will be utilized to identify struggling students and why they are struggling. • Interventions matched to student needs will result in student learning increases for all students. • All students at risk of low achievement	*Who is in charge of RtI?* Cindy Smith, RtI Coordinator *Who is on the RtI Team?* RtI Coordinator Student Services Coordinator Principal Counselors Curriculum Coordinator Instructional Coaches General & Special Education Teachers *Purpose of the RtI Team* The purpose of the RtI Team is to lead and monitor the implementation of RtI with integrity and fidelity throughout the school. (See RtI Team Roles and Responsibilities.) Multiple Teams might be used.	• Teachers in their grade level teams determine what they are going to teach, and the materials they are going to use. • All students are screened within two weeks of school starting in their core classroom, and again at the middle and end of the year. • The results of the screeners are reviewed by the RtI Team to get a schoolwide view of the performance of all students, set cut scores, and allocate support. • RtI Team reviews the screening results with classroom teachers to confirm risk and together set up interventions for students at risk of failing. • Secondary Intervention is provided for 30 minutes, 5 days per week for 9 to 15 weeks for students in groups of 5 to 8. • Tertiary Intervention is provided for 40 minutes per day in groups of 1 to 4, for 9 – 15 weeks. • After the initial screening, classroom teachers may make a request to the RtI Team that other students be assigned to secondary or tertiary interventions, based on teacher observations, progress monitoring data, mastery tests, and formative checks. • Instruction for interventions is provided by interventionists, classroom teachers, special education teachers, resource teachers, push-in teachers, or other staff, as determined by the RtI Team.	The RtI and Curriculum Coordinators support implementation with direction, observation, and feedback that is shared only with the classroom teacher, providing other support as requested. *How should implementation be monitored?* Administrators conduct fidelity checks through observations, using a classroom and intervention observation tool. *To what degree is RtI being implemented with fidelity?* RtI components are known and most are implemented with fidelity. Teachers need to improve independent working strategies for small group instruction techniques.	State Standards Assessment results will be used to: • show instructional coherence. • indicate student proficiency and learning growth. Universal screening data from beginning, middle, and end of year will be reviewed to see how numbers of students in need of interventions change over time. Numbers of students who exit Secondary and Tertiary Level Preventions will be monitored and reviewed to see if the numbers exiting increases over time and is the result of effective interventions. Demographic data will be used to follow: • Retentions • Failures • Attendance • Discipline referrals • Requests for evaluation • Evaluations completed	State Standards Assessments will show instructional coherence and indicate student proficiency with student scores similarly high regardless of teacher. Universal screening data will show decreasing numbers of students in need of Secondary and Tertiary Levels of Prevention from beginning of the year to end of the year. Number of students exiting Secondary and Tertiary Levels will decrease over time due to effectiveness of interventions. Demographic data will show a decrease or consistently low numbers for: • Retentions • Failures • Attendance • Discipline referrals • Requests for evaluation • Evaluations completed • Number of students found eligible for special education Perception data will reflect agreement at high rates on favorable perception on morale,

Figure 4.2 *(Continued)*
Our School's System of Response to Intervention

NEEDS	PURPOSE OF RtI		LEADS		IMPLEMENTATION		EVALUATION	
What Are Your Needs Assessment Results?	*What Is the Purpose of RtI?*	*Who is RtI Intending to Serve?*	*What Are the Desired Outcomes for RtI?*	*Who Leads RtI?*	*What Will RtI Look Like When Fully Implemented with Integrity and Fidelity?*	*How Is RtI Implementation Being Monitored?*	*How Will Results Be Measured?*	*What Are the Results?*
Students in upper grade levels do not feel challenged by the work they are asked to do. Students feel other students' behavior gets in the way of their learning. Teachers feel student behavior needs to improve. Teachers do not work together to create a continuum of learning. Not all teachers believe that using data will improve student learning. Teachers say they believe all students can learn.	environment, with access to the general education content, materials, and expectations. • Ensure the appropriate identification of students with special needs.	All students within the general education setting.	are identified early and "failure" is prevented. • Referrals made for evaluation of special education are accurate. • Fewer students will be identified for special education. • Students will not be placed in special education for the wrong reasons, such as teachers wanting students out of the classroom because of behavior or lack of learning response, poor test-taking skills, second language learning, or lack of adequate interventions. • Attendance and student engagement will improve because we are meeting the needs of *every* student. • Behavior will improve because we are engaging *all* students in learning.	They will work together to ensure a systemic view and implementation of RtI, with integrity and fidelity throughout the school.	• *Every* students' progress is monitored weekly at secondary and tertiary levels using identified progress monitoring tools. • Teachers analyze assessment results in data teams and determine how to improve instruction to reach *all* students. • If students are not making progress after 4 to 6 data points, the interventions may be changed, if the current interventions have been implemented with integrity and fidelity. RtI Team will monitor and ensure integrity and fidelity of implementation. • All interventions and student responses are documented. • All instruction and intervention is monitored for fidelity of implementation. • The system of RtI is evaluated for implementation integrity, fidelity and effectiveness. • Implementation is shown in flowcharting format reflecting the system and the classroom or individual student.		• Number of students found eligible for special education. Perception data will be used to assess student, staff, and parent perceptions about learning, morale, and the system of RtI. Perception data will be used to assess staff knowledge and understanding of • RtI components. • Implementation of the system for RtI. • Purpose and intent of RtI. • Our school's mission and vision. Process data will be used through collaborative staff meetings to review and monitor instructional coherence expectations and outcomes; confirmed through observations.	student learning, and the system of RtI for parents, students, and staff. Staff surveys specific to the system of RtI will show high levels of agreement and high levels of competence for: • Identifying the components of RtI. • Understanding the purpose and intent of RtI. • Applying our school vision and mission to the system of RtI. • Identifying implementation procedures for the system of RtI. Teachers have gained strategies for meeting the needs of our students reflected in all assessment results indicating sustained learning growth for *every* student, in *every* grade, in *every* classroom.

NEXT STEPS
Implementation monitoring data show that teachers need professional learning and coaching in the following:
   • Analyzing data to determine student needs.
   • Differentiating instruction to meet students' needs.
   • Adjusting instruction to enable strategic small group instruction and to keep the other students working independently.
Classroom teachers and interventionists need more time to plan together so that interventions transfer to classroom instruction.

Components of the System of Responsive Interventions

Many details need to be addressed within each of these components of RtI; specifically, plans for the universal screener, progress monitor, and the multi-level prevention system need to identify tools you will use, how to strengthen *Primary Prevention* when working at a school with a predominance of at-risk students, who is going to administer or be in charge of each component, how are you going to use the information, and how will it be monitored.

Schoolwide Assessment Inventory

Many assessments are used in a school system, including, but not limited to, the following:

- ◆ Achievement Tests
- ◆ Common Formative Assessments
- ◆ Diagnostic Assessments
- ◆ Placement Tests
- ◆ Progress Monitors
- ◆ State and Districtwide Assessments
- ◆ Teacher Made Assessments
- ◆ Unit Assessments
- ◆ Universal Screeners

As RtI-specific assessments are identified and put into place, it is important to review the assessments used throughout the school. A Schoolwide Assessment Inventory, such as Figure 4.3, helps staff identify all the assessments used in the school, and how they are used. The Schoolwide Assessment Inventory will allow staff to determine which assessments are supporting their efforts, where there is overlap, and what is missing. The Schoolwide Assessment Inventory also appears as RtI Implementation Guide #8. Use this to lay out all assessments in your school.

*Many details need to be addressed within each of these components of RtI; specifically, plans for the universal screener, progress monitor, and the multi-level prevention system need to identify tools you will use, how to strengthen **Primary Prevention** when working at a school with a predominance of at-risk students, who is going to administer or be in charge of each component, how you are going to use the information, and how it will it be monitored.*

*The **Schoolwide Assessment Inventory** will allow staff to determine which assessments are supporting their efforts, where there is overlap, and what is missing.*

Figure 4.3
Schoolwide Assessment Inventory

SUBJECT:

ASSESSMENT NAME (e.g., DIBELS)	TARGETED ASSESSMENT AREA (e.g., Reading Fluency)	DATES OF COLLECTION AND LENGTH OF ASSESSMENT (e.g., date or number of times administered, for how long)	GRADE LEVEL(S)	WHO HAS ACCESS TO RESULTS?	USES					COMMENTS
					Screening	Diagnostics	Instruction—Imbedded	Progress Monitoring	Summative	

RtI relies on two types of assessments to identify and monitor students at risk for poor learning outcomes: Universal Screeners and Progress Monitors. Information from these assessments is used in conjunction with other school assessments to inform instruction and intervention across prevention levels.

Universal Screeners
Universal screening is conducted to identify or predict students who may be at risk for poor learning outcomes. Universal screeners in academic performance are frequent, brief, reliable, valid, accurate predictors of risk, and sensitive to small amounts of growth. They measure essential skills for accessing curriculum and instruction (i.e., read, write, compute). Universal screeners must be aligned with the curriculum/what you want students to know and be able to do, administered to all students at least three times a year, usually at the beginning, middle, and end of the year, and may be followed by additional testing or short-term progress monitoring to corroborate students' risk status.

Universal screeners specifically for behavior may take the form of a standardized assessment instrument, usually a checklist, completed by teachers for every student, or may be in the form of a process involving nominations paired with monitoring key data such as discipline and attendance. Universal screening procedures for both academic and behavior RtI should not take more than 30 minutes to administer per content area, and they should be monitored for *integrity* and *fidelity* of implementation.

Universal screeners are used to identify students at or above a cut point (e.g., at or above grade level) who will continue to receive Primary Prevention; students below the cut point who will be considered for Secondary Prevention along with Primary Prevention; and students significantly below the cut point who will be considered for Tertiary Prevention along with Primary Prevention. Sometimes in early grades, especially Kindergarten, a large percentage of students – maybe even 80% – perform below the cut point. This is not a result of poor core instruction. This might be a result of little or no experience with school, English, or reading. However, if 80% of 4th graders perform below the cut point, this may be the result of poor core instruction.

Cut point, or the score on the assessment that differentiates who is in need of intervention and who is not, is used to inform decisions regarding assignment to prevention levels. The RtI Team should begin with recommendations from the screener and assessment tools being used as well as consider the school's learning and performance profile as identified from a review of the schoolwide data. Once the initial list of students in need of Secondary or Tertiary Intervention is generated, RtI teams will need to confirm risk

Universal screening is conducted to identify or predict students who may be at risk for poor learning outcomes.

*Universal screeners are used to identify students at or above a cut point (e.g., at or above grade level) who will continue to receive **Primary Prevention;** students below the cut point who will be considered for **Secondary Prevention** along with **Primary Prevention;** and students significantly below the cut point who will be considered for **Tertiary Prevention** along with **Primary Prevention.***

When data indicate a large number of students in need of intervention, teachers should study and learn new strategies for creating a stronger instructional match at the **Primary Prevention Level.**

Use **RtI Implementation Guide #9** to spell out the details related to your school's procedures and use of academic universal screeners.

Use **PBIS Implementation Guide #24** to spell out the details related to your school's procedures and use of PBIS universal screeners.

status prior to assignment to intervention by taking into consideration prior performance and interventions, teacher observations, and the support the school has to cover the intervention. When data indicate a large number of students in need of intervention, teachers should study and learn new strategies for creating a stronger instructional match at the Primary Prevention Level.

Figure 4.4 shows how one staff thought through the details of identifying, implementing, monitoring, and evaluating their school's *Universal Screener,* using RtI Implementation Guide #9, *Our School Universal Screeners.* Use RtI Implementation Guide #9 to spell out the details related to your school's procedures and use of academic *Universal Screeners.* Use PBIS Implementation Guide #24 to spell out the details related to your school's procedures and use of *PBIS Universal Screeners.*

Figure 4.4
Our School Universal Screeners

Components	What tool(s)?	How many times a year is it administered? When is it administered?	Who administers it?	How is it administered? To whom is it administered?	Who scores the tests?	Who interprets the results?	How are the results shared with Teachers? Students? Parents?	What are the cut points? How are cut points identified?	Additional sources to confirm student risk status?	How will you know this tool will accurately classify students?
Reading	◆ Universal Screener Name	Three times a year: ◆ Beginning of the school year; ◆ Middle of the school year; ◆ End of the school year	◆ All classroom teachers.	◆ Laptops in classroom. ◆ All students.	◆ Computer-based.	◆ RtI Team initially to get a systemic view of the scores. ◆ RtI team with classroom teachers.	◆ RtI Team and individual classroom teachers, then schoolwide.	◆ To be determined by RtI Team, in conjunction with classroom teachers, and screener recommended cut points.	◆ Classroom performance, previous years' performance and interventions, CBM Diagnostics, and Progress Monitoring probes.	◆ Review the end of year results, teacher input, and previous year's scores.

Progress monitoring is used to assess a student's performance and quantify her or his rate of improvement and responsiveness to intervention, to adjust the student's intervention intensity, to make it more effective and suited to the student's needs, and to evaluate the effectiveness of the intervention.

RtI Implementation Guide #10, Our School Progress Monitors, guides staff in thinking through the details of identifying, planning for, implementing, monitoring, and evaluating progress monitors for academic RtI.

PBIS Implementation Guide #25, Our School Progress Monitors in PBIS, guides staff through the details of identifying, planning for, implementing, monitoring, and evaluating progress monitors for PBIS.

Progress Monitors

Progress monitoring is used to assess a student's performance and quantify her or his rate of improvement and responsiveness to intervention, to adjust the student's intervention intensity, to make it more effective and suited to the student's needs, and to evaluate the effectiveness of the intervention.

Like *Universal Screeners, Progress Monitors* are brief, valid, reliable, accurate predictors of risk, and sensitive to small amounts of growth; however, they are more frequent. *Progress Monitors* need to align with the curriculum and what you want students to know and be able to do, as well as inform the team about the effectiveness of interventions. *Progress Monitors* are administered to students in Secondary and Tertiary Prevention Levels at regular intervals, often weekly, to quantify short- and long-term student gains, and usually take 5 to 15 minutes to administer. While they are similar to *Universal Screeners, Progress Monitors* are ongoing measures of essential skills that allow access to curriculum and instruction, provide continuous feedback to both the student and the teacher concerning learning successes and failures, and can be both formal and informal measures of student progress. For behavior, *Progress Monitoring* often involves charting or graphing the results from a daily behavior report card or behavior chart. It may also involve a daily or weekly rating by adults for specific behaviors. For both academic and behavior concerns, *Progress Monitors* identify students who are and are not demonstrating adequate rates of improvement so changes can be made. The administration and uses of *Progress Monitors* need to be monitored to ensure implementation with integrity and fidelity.

Progress monitoring results are best reviewed in graph form with specific features to help with decisions, described in Chapter 6. These graphs will provide the information needed for RtI Teams to determine if students are making substantial, sufficient, questionable, or poor progress. If *progress monitoring* data indicate that a student is not making adequate progress or demonstrates such slow learning growth after multiple interventions, she or he may be referred for consideration of further evaluation provided the student has received two or more interventions with consistency and fidelity.

RtI Implementation Guide #10, *Our School Progress Monitors,* partially shown in Figure 4.5, guides staff in thinking through the details of identifying, planning for, implementing, monitoring, and evaluating *Progress Monitors* for academic RtI. PBIS Implementation Guide #25, *Our School Progress Monitors for PBIS,* guides staff through the details of identifying, planning for, implementing, monitoring, and evaluating *Progress Monitors* for PBIS.

Figure 4.5
Our School Progress Monitors

Components	What tool(s)?	When are the assessments administered?	Who administers the assessments?	How are they administered?	Who scores the assessments?	Who interprets results?	How are results shared with teachers, students, and parents?	How are aimlines determined?	How is growth monitored?	How do you know these tools accurately show student growth?
Reading - *Primary Prevention (Formative Assessment)*	• *Core Curriculum* • State Standards Assessment • Unit tests; Classroom Assessment; Universal Screening	• Formative and summative for each lesson or unit. • Benchmark test: Quarterly. • Universal Screener-Beginning, middle and end of year.	• Classroom Teachers	• Paper-pencil • Computer	• Classroom Teachers • Computer • State	• Teachers in Data Teams	• Schoolwide – share out by Data Team. • Share with students in classroom. • Reports to Parents.	• NA	• Classroom Teachers review data in Data Teams.	• Look at the results of all measures together. • Review monitoring data for integrity and fidelity of implementation.
Reading - *Strategic/ Secondary Intervention*	• Our School Progress Monitoring Tool	• Weekly	• Classroom Teachers	• Computer	• Computer	• Teachers in Data Teams • RtI Team	• Schoolwide – share out by Data Team. • Share with students. • Share progress with parents.	• Computer provides, with teacher input for goal.	• Classroom Teachers review data in Data Teams. • RtI Team reviews every 4-6 weeks for intervention effectiveness.	• Look at the results of all measures together. • Review monitoring data for integrity and fidelity of implementation.
Reading - *Intensive/Tertiary Intervention*	• Our School Progress Monitoring Tool	• Weekly	• Classroom Teachers	• Computer	• Computer	• Teachers in Data Teams • RtI Team	• Schoolwide – share out by Data Team. • Share with students. • Share progress with parents.	• Computer Provides with teacher input for goal.	• Classroom Teachers review data in Data Teams. • RtI Team reviews every 4-6 weeks for intervention effectiveness.	• Look at the results of all measures together. • Review monitoring data for integrity and fidelity of implementation.

Multi-Level Prevention System

The *Multi-Level Prevention System* usually consists of three levels:

- *Primary Prevention, Level One,* or *Core Instruction;*
- *Secondary Prevention, Level Two,* or *Strategic Intervention;*
- *Tertiary Prevention, Level Three,* or *Intensive Intervention.*

Primary Prevention, Level One: Core Instruction

The most efficient and effective way to ensure learning growth for *every* student is to provide high quality instruction, in every classroom at *every* grade level, aligned to what you want students to know and be able to do, otherwise known as *instructional coherence.* The quality of *Primary Level Prevention* will greatly influence the number of students in need of *Secondary and Tertiary Intervention.*

Every student receives high quality core instruction that is aligned to the state's achievement standards, is culturally responsive, and is research and evidence-based. When a teacher is providing high quality core instruction that is designed specifically for her/his students' abilities, the instruction should be reaching at least 80% of the students, 100% of the time.

Primary Prevention:

- Is provided to all students, including those receiving Secondary and Tertiary Prevention.
- Involves high quality core curriculum and instruction that is researched-based, implemented with *integrity and fidelity,* designed to meet the needs of most students.
- Involves implementation of curriculum that is monitored to ensure instructional coherence.
- Includes evidence-based materials and practices to teach grade level standards and expectations.
- Regardless of the make up of the school (high-risk, high-poverty, highly-transient, etc.), Primary Prevention must be adjusted to meet the needs of 80% of students.
- Involves instructional practices that are culturally responsive.
- Involves Universal Design for Learning (UDL) to accommodate the needs of diverse learners and ensure access to instruction by all students.
- Includes differentiated learning activities to address individual learning differences.

The most efficient and effective way to ensure learning growth for every student is to provide high quality instruction, in every classroom at every grade level, aligned to what you want students to know and be able to do, otherwise known as instructional coherence.

*The quality of **Primary Level Prevention** will greatly influence the number of students in need of **Secondary** and **Tertiary Intervention.***

*Primary Prevention is provided to all students at all times, including those receiving **Secondary** and **Tertiary Levels** of Prevention.*

- Includes formative assessments that are administered to *all* students to determine student growth over time.
- Includes universal screening to determine students' current level of performance and identify students at risk for poor learning outcomes and therefore in need of additional levels of prevention.

Primary Prevention also includes and requires strategically designed instruction in order to meet the needs of most of the students, *all* of the time. When teachers do not realize the need to provide for an instructional match at the Primary Level, even when that means providing what other teachers provide as intervention, we often see the upside down pyramid, or inverted triangle, with too many students in need of intervention.

One page of RtI Implementation Guide #11, *Our School Primary Prevention, Level One: Core Instruction,* is shown in Figure 4.6. Use this RtI tool to design your high quality Primary Prevention. This information subsequently will assist with the monitoring and evaluation of Core Instruction. Use PBIS Implementation Guide #26, *Our School PBIS Primary Prevention, Level One: Universal Strategies,* to design your PBIS Primary Prevention.

Primary Prevention also includes and requires strategically designed instruction in order to meet the needs of most of the students, all of the time. When teachers do not realize the need to provide for an instructional match at the Primary Level, even when that means providing what other teachers provide as intervention, we often see the upside down pyramid, or inverted triangle, with too many students in need of intervention.

Use **RtI Implementation Guide #11, Our School Primary Prevention, Level One: Core Instruction,** *to design your high quality Primary Prevention.*

Use **PBIS Implementation Guide #26, Our School PBIS Primary Prevention, Level One: Universal Strategies,** *to design your* **PBIS Primary Prevention**

Figure 4.6
Our School Primary Prevention, Level One: Core Instruction

What curriculum?	Instructor	Length of time and instructional strategies	Setting	Progress Monitoring, frequency	Sources to determine student is at risk?	Integrity and Fidelity Monitoring	Additional support
◆ Core developed from Scientifically Based Reading Research.	◆ Classroom Teacher. ◆ Co-taught with special education teacher ◆ Support from literacy aides.	◆ 90 minutes per day minimum (60 minutes maximum whole group; 30 minutes minimum small group). ◆ Teachers provide UDL and differentiated instruction for whole group, small group, work stations, and direct, explicit instruction for the essential areas of reading: phonemic awareness, phonics, fluency, comprehension, and vocabulary.	◆ Classroom	◆ Mastery tests, unit tests, and weekly/bi-weekly common grade level formative assessments.	◆ Universal Screener, previous performance, teacher observation, Progress Monitoring.	◆ The Curriculum Coordinator supports implementation with direction, observation, and feedback that is shared only with the classroom teacher and relevant data teams. ◆ Principal and Curriculum Coordinator conduct fidelity checks in collaborative meetings with teachers and direct observations.	◆ Teachers meet in Data Teams to review student performance and discuss improving instruction. ◆ Collaborative teams meet to review delivery of curriculum and instruction; using checklists for discussion of integrity and fidelity to monitor instructional coherence with the Curriculum Coordinator.

Secondary Prevention, Level Two: Strategic Intervention
Students who need additional and strategic support are offered *Secondary Prevention.*

Students who need additional and strategic support are provided **Secondary Prevention.**

Secondary Prevention has at least four distinguishing characteristics:

1. It is evidence-based;

2. Typically relies on adult-led, small-group instruction rather than whole-class instruction to address a student's area of risk or low performance;

3. It involves a clearly articulated, validated intervention, matched to student needs which should be adhered to with *integrity and fidelity;* and

4. It does not include repetition of core instruction at just a slower rate.

Secondary Prevention:

- Is in addition to, never in place of, *Primary Prevention.*

- Typically relies entirely on adult-led small-group instruction rather than whole-class instruction.

- Involves small-group instruction (5 to 8 students).

- Is typically 9 to 15 weeks of 20- to 30-minute sessions, 3 to 5 times per week (half a semester in length, minimum).

- Involves a clearly articulated, validated intervention, consistently adhered to with *integrity and fidelity,* aligned with *Primary Prevention,* and designed to target identified areas of risk.

- Diagnostic assessments may be used to better identify targeted areas for instruction and intervention.

- Refers to targeted supplemental instruction and intervention that is evidence-based.

- Is expected to benefit a large majority of students who do not respond to effective *Primary Prevention.*

- Is aimed at remediating the identified areas of risk or poor performance for students who fail to meet expected benchmarks so they can be successful in *Primary* or *Core Instruction.*

*Secondary Prevention is in addition to, never in place of, **Primary Prevention.***

Decisions regarding change of interventions due to unresponsiveness will consider the length of intervention, number and consistency of sessions, and sufficient data to demonstrate the current intervention is not effective and will not yield desired results if maintained with integrity and fidelity.

Decisions regarding change of interventions due to unresponsiveness will consider the length of intervention, number and consistency of sessions, and sufficient data to demonstrate the current intervention is not effective and will not yield desired results if maintained with integrity and fidelity.

*RtI Implementation Guide #12, Our School Secondary Prevention, Level Two: Strategic Intervention, a guide for designing high quality Secondary Prevention Level or Strategic Intervention. Use this tool to design, implement, monitor, and evaluate your school's **Secondary Prevention.***

*Use **PBIS Implementation Guide #27, Our School PBIS Secondary Prevention, Level Two: Strategic Intervention,** to design, implement, monitor, and evaluate your school's PBIS Secondary Prevention.*

Figure 4.7 shows one page of the example taken from RtI Implementation Guide #12, *Our School Secondary Prevention, Level Two: Strategic Intervention,* a guide for designing high quality *Secondary Prevention Level* or *Strategic Intervention.* Use this tool to design, implement, monitor, and evaluate your school's Secondary Prevention. Use PBIS Implementation Guide #27, *Our School PBIS Secondary Prevention, Level Two: Strategic Intervention,* to design, implement, monitor, and evaluate your school's PBIS *Secondary Prevention.*

Figure 4.7
Our School Secondary Prevention, Level Two: Strategic Intervention

Specific Intervention/ Materials used.	Number of students in the group / Type of instruction / Location	Number of intervention sessions / Frequency of sessions / Length of sessions	Instructor: Who will provide the intervention instruction	Support: Additional personnel and resources	Progress Monitoring tool and frequency of administration	Criteria for Exit from intervention / Exit to additional tertiary intervention / Referral for consideration of evaluation	Integrity and Fidelity Monitoring
◆ Evidence-based interventions for targeted area of risk in one or more of five essential reading components. Check one: ☒ Standard Protocol: ☐ Problem Solving ◆ Supplemental program that accompanies our Core Reading Program.	◆ Small groups: 5 to 8 students. ◆ Students grouped by similar instructional needs and outcomes. ◆ Location: general education classroom with Teaching Assistant support.	◆ Daily sessions ◆ 30 minute sessions ◆ 9 weeks minimum, with acceptable progress. (Change before 9 weeks if poor progress).	◆ Classroom teachers with part time teachers. ◆ In general education classroom.	◆ Part-Time Teachers. ◆ Curriculum Coaches. ◆ Special Education teachers for intervention strategies.	◆ Progress monitoring probe (10 minutes maximum) on the computer. ◆ Every Wednesday. ◆ Administered in classrooms.	◆ Review by RtI team using trendline analysis after 6 weeks of intervention. 1) Student making substantial progress- exit from Secondary Prevention level. 2) Student making sufficient progress- continue Secondary Prevention as is. 3) Student making questionable or poor progress- move to Tertiary Prevention. 4) After two intervention cycles with poor progress, document all interventions and responses, then consult Student Services Coordinator regarding referral procedures.	◆ The Curriculum Coordinator supports implementation with direction, observation, and feedback that is shared only with the classroom teacher and relevant data teams. Curriculum coordinator also meets with collaborative teams to review integrity and fidelity checklists, and discuss instructional coherence. ◆ Administrators conduct observations for integrity and fidelity.

*Tertiary Prevention is the most intensive of the three levels and is provided with **integrity** and **fidelity** in very small homogenous groups or individualized to target each student's area(s) of need.*

Tertiary Prevention, Level Three: Intensive Intervention
Tertiary Prevention is the most intensive of the three levels and is provided with *integrity* and *fidelity* in very small, homogenous groups or individualized to target each student's area(s) of need. Intensity may be added in one of the following ways:

- Decreasing group size.

- Increasing session frequency.

- Increasing session length.

- Changing to a more explicit or direct instruction intervention with very frequent feedback and error correction (often requires small group size to be effective).

*Tertiary Prevention is in addition to, never in place of, **Primary Instruction**. May result from lack of response to **Secondary Intervention**.*

Tertiary Prevention:

- Is in addition to, never in place of, *Primary Instruction.*

- May result from lack of response to *Secondary Intervention.*

- Typically has 1 to 4 students in a group.

- Is typically 9 to 15 weeks of 30–40 minute sessions, daily.

- Involves a clearly articulated, validated intervention consistently adhered to with *integrity and fidelity* and designed to target identified areas of risk.

- Focuses on students who have not responded to *Primary and Secondary Preventions,* or who have very low achievement on *Universal Screeners* (two or more grade levels below expected performance).

- May begin with a more intensive version of the intervention approach used in *Secondary Prevention* (e.g., longer sessions, smaller group size, more frequent sessions).

- Diagnostic assessments may be used to better identify targeted areas for instruction and intervention.

- Before a team decides that a student who has been receiving Strategic Interventions requires Intensive Intervention in a certain content area, the team should consider whether or not the student has received *Secondary Prevention* with integrity and fidelity.

- If progress monitoring assessments indicate that a student is not making adequate progress, she or he may be referred for further evaluation provided the student has consistently received more than one intervention program with integrity and fidelity.

- Requires documentation of intervention and student's response.

Figure 4.8 shows one page of the example taken from RtI Implementation Guide #13, *Our School Tertiary Prevention, Level Three: Intensive Intervention,* a tool for designing high quality *Tertiary Prevention Level or Intensive, Intervention.* Use this tool to design, implement, monitor, and evaluate your school's *Tertiary Prevention.* Use PBIS Implementation Guide #28, *Our School PBIS Tertiary Prevention, Level Three: Intensive Intervention,* to design, implement, monitor, and evaluate your school's PBIS Tertiary Prevention.

Use *RtI Implementation Guide #13, Our School Tertiary Prevention, Level Three* to design, implement, monitor, and evaluate your school's Tertiary Prevention.

Use *PBIS Implementation Guide #28, Our School PBIS Tertiary Prevention, Level Three* to design, implement, monitor, and evaluate your school's PBIS Tertiary Prevention.

Figure 4.8
Our School Tertiary Prevention, Level Three: Intensive Intervention

Specific Intervention/ Materials used.	Number of students in group / Type of instruction / Location of Intervention	Number of intervention sessions / Frequency of sessions / Length of sessions	Instructor: Who will provide the intervention instruction	Support: Additional personnel and resources	Progress Monitoring tool and frequency of administration	Criteria for Exit from intervention. Exit to additional tertiary intervention. Referral for consideration of evaluation	Integrity and Fidelity Monitoring
◆ Evidence-based interventions to target area of risk. Check one: ☐ Standard Treatment ☒ Problem solving	◆ 3 Students in small group or individual instruction. ◆ Students grouped by similar instructional needs and outcomes. ◆ Location: general education classroom.	◆ 12 weeks of sessions, minimum, if making progress. ◆ Daily sessions. ◆ 30 minutes in small groups; at least 20 minutes if individual.	◆ Instruction provided by classroom teacher or specialist trained to provide intervention.	◆ Part-time teachers. ◆ Special Education teacher or specialists can provide intervention strategy ideas.	◆ Weekly Assessments using Progress Monitoring probes from Screener system.	◆ Review by RtI team using trendline analysis after 6 weeks of intervention. 1) Student making substantial progress-exit from Secondary Prevention. 2) Student making sufficient progress-continue Secondary Prevention as is. 3) Student making questionable or poor progress? Increase intensity or change intervention. 4) After two intervention cycles with poor progress, document all interventions and responses, then consult Student Services Coordinator regarding referral procedures.	◆ The Curriculum Coordinator supports implementation with direction, observation, and feedback that is shared only with the classroom teacher and relevant data teams. Curriculum coordinator also meets with collaborative teams to review integrity and fidelity checklists, and discuss instructional coherence. ◆ Administrators conduct observations for integrity and fidelity.

Roles and Responsibilities

RtI implemented with *integrity* and *fidelity* calls for new and expanded roles for every staff member. For RtI to be successful, each role needs to be clearly identified with specific RtI responsibilities.

*RtI implemented with **integrity** and **fidelity** calls for new and expanded roles for every staff member.*

Roles to be defined for successful implementation include all staff members and Leadership Teams. Major RtI responsibilities include:

- ◆ Assessment
- ◆ Instruction
- ◆ Interventions
- ◆ Data Analysis
- ◆ Collaboration
- ◆ Evaluate Program/Services
- ◆ Evaluate Student Performance

Figure 4.9 shows one page of example roles and responsibilities from *RtI Implementation Guide #14, Primary Roles and Responsibilities in Our School System of RtI.* Use this form to identify the Roles and Responsibilities for your school's System of RtI.

*Use **RtI Implementation Guide #14, Primary Roles and Responsibilities in Our School System of RtI** to identify the Roles and Responsibilities for your school's System of RtI.*

Figure 4.9

Primary Roles and Responsibilities in Our School System of RtI

What is the role of...	In... Assessment (Universal Screener, Progress Monitoring)	Instruction	Intervention	Data Analysis	Collaboration	Evaluation of Programs and Services	Evaluating Student Performance (Secondary or Tertiary Prevention)
RtI Coordinator	• Work with the RtI Teams to review Universal Screener and Progress Monitor data, schoolwide, and with individual teachers.	• Support general educators via consultation, push in, direct instruction, modeling, and monitoring progress and documentation.	• Deliver Tertiary sessions. • Coordinate computer-assisted interventions. • Manage student enrollment in Prevention levels (computer). • Assist with documentation.	• Collect and organize data. • Use data tools. • Participate in analysis as a member of a Data Team. • Work with RtI Teams to match results with interventions.	• Collaborate to plan for instruction and intervention, using data. • Provide support in area(s) of expertise. • Collaborate to coordinate intervention schedule(s) as needed.	• Assist in gathering process and program effectiveness data for analysis and improvement. • Contribute additional intervention ideas.	• Collect data on students who receive Tertiary Interventions. • Team member for determining acceptable progress and next steps.
RtI Team – Academic and Behavioral	• Set assessment schedule. • Review, organize, and analyze screening results; adjust cut scores; take into account previous scores and interventions; share results with teachers. • Oversee the activities of RtI.	• Support general education teachers to deliver high quality core curriculum to all students. • Collaborate with teachers to monitor instructional coherence. • Coordinate and communicate with PLCs and other teams.	• Schedule interventions and support. • Align student needs with resources and interventions. • Monitor for integrity and fidelity. • Assist with maintaining necessary documentation.	• Review Universal Screener and Progress Monitor data, schoolwide and with individual teachers. • Set goals for students assigned to Prevention levels, using data to gauge for realistic but ambitious goals. • Oversee the activities of RtI Teams.	• Collaborate with homeroom teachers, content area teachers, and intervention teachers to plan instruction and interventions. • Collaborate with teachers to monitor instructional coherence.	• Design and conduct program evaluation. • Analyze for improvements. • Ensure integrity and fidelity of implementation.	• Review universal screening and progress monitoring data with homeroom teachers, content area teachers, and intervention teachers to determine student growth, acceptable progress, and next steps.

RtI Team

More details are needed to define the *Roles and Responsibilities of the RtI Team.* Who will lead the design, implementation, monitoring, and evaluation of RtI throughout the school? Who will be on this team? Who can make sure the RtI plan is carried out with integrity and fidelity? The recommendation is that the Principal NOT be the *RtI Coordinator.* Schools need someone who will be available to staff, students, and parents, not pulled out for meetings, disciplinary issues, etc., and has the skills and time to ponder the whole system, while considering each classroom's needs. Figure 4.10 is one page of *RtI Implementation Guide #15, Response to Intervention (RtI) Team Purpose, Roles, and Responsibilities,* that shows how one school defined the purpose and roles and responsibilities of its team. Use this tool to define your school's *RtI Team Purpose, Roles and Responsibilities*. In large schools, it might be feasible to have more than one RtI Team. These schools must take additional steps to establish communication that will ensure a systemic view of RtI at all times.

RtI Implementation Guide #15, RtI Response to Intervention (RtI) Team Purpose, Roles, and Responsibilities, shows how one school defined the purpose, and roles and responsibilities of its team.

Figure 4.10
Purpose, Roles, and Responsibilities for the RtI Team

RESPONSE TO INTERVENTION (RtI) TEAM PURPOSE, ROLES, AND RESPONSIBILITIES

The RtI Team is composed of:

- RtI Coordinator
- Curriculum Coordinator
- Student Services Coordinator
- Principal
- Assistant Principal
- Counselors
- Instructional Coach(es)
- General and Special Education Teachers

The purpose of the RtI Team is to lead and monitor the implementation of RtI with integrity and fidelity throughout the school. Larger schools may have more than one RtI team. Multiple RtI teams must meet and communicate regularly to ensure instructional coherence throughout the school.

RtI Teams will:
- Set the assessment schedule.
- Review, organize, and analyze universal screening results, schoolwide, to recommend students for Secondary and Tertiary Prevention (intervention) levels.
- After reviewing the schoolwide screening data in view of intervention possibilities, adjust cut scores; share results with teachers and interventionists.
- Confirm risk status and assign students to interventions taking into account previous scores and interventions.
- Set up intervention schedules, set goals to establish aimlines for all students in interventions.
- Collaborate with classroom teachers, content area teachers, and intervention teachers to ensure our core instruction meets the needs of 80% or more of our students.
- Support general education teachers to deliver core curriculum with coherence.
- Collaborate with classroom teachers, content area teachers, and intervention teachers to plan instruction and interventions.
- Review progress-monitoring data with classroom teachers to consider changes in assignment to intervention levels.
- Ensure documentation of interventions and student responsiveness for those at risk for referral to special education (pre-referral documentation).
- Monitor students who access Secondary or Tertiary interventions from year to year for coordination of appropriate interventions and decisions regarding referral for consideration of evaluation.

Positions that are set up to support classroom teachers need further detail so there is no confusion of roles and purposes. Figure 4.11 outlines one way to define responsibilities for the support personnel. Figure 4.11 is also *RtI Implementation Guide #16, RtI Support Protocol for Curriculum Coach: What I Will, May, and Won't Do When I Come into Your Classroom.* **Note,** *PBIS Implementation Guide #29, Support Protocol for Behavior Specialist: What I Will, May, and Won't Do When I Come into Your Classroom,* **is an** example support protocol for PBIS.

Use RtI Implementation Guide #16, RtI Support Protocol for Curriculum Coach: What I Will, May, and Won't Do When I Come into Your Classroom to outline responsibilities of support personnel.

Figure 4.11
RtI Support Protocol Example

What I will do...	What I may do...	What I won't do...
Visit your classroom during instruction.	Model lessons in your classroom.	Evaluate your performance as a teacher.
Collaborate with you to set goals for improving instruction during Professional Learning Community/ Data Team Meetings.	Assist you in organizing and interpreting progress monitoring data.	Give written notes/ observations to anyone except you (the teacher).
Provide support and assistance with instruction, assessment, and data analysis.	Provide on-site training during Data Team Meetings related to instruction.	Interrupt your instructional time by conferencing or discussing observations during instruction.
Meet with you regularly to address questions, share information, etc.	Make recommendations of resources to enhance or supplement your instruction.	Supervise students or provide ongoing instruction, except when modeling.
Assist in generalizing Strategic Interventions into Primary Level Prevention to avoid intervention conflict.	Assist with flexible grouping of students, based on data, at the Primary Prevention level.	Just 'hang out' or make copies.
Assist you in implementing progress monitoring in your classroom as well as critical elements of instruction that are shared at professional learning sessions and team meetings.	Assist with design of differentiated lessons based on your classroom data.	
Serve as your guide in implementing a Schoolwide Prevention System with integrity and fidelity.	Assist with planning Universal Design for Learning (UDL) activities in your classroom.	
Answer any questions you may have about our Prevention System and curricula. (If I don't know, I will find out, and get back to you.)	Retrain or model to improve integrity and fidelity of implementation for curriculum and assessments.	
Participate in evaluation of core, supplemental, and intervention materials/programs.		
Monitor integrity and fidelity by observing pacing in the core curriculum, Universal Screening, Progress Monitoring, and intervention sessions.		

Data Teams provide another system of support. Align your current Data Team purpose and responsibilities to ensure implementation of your system of RtI, with integrity and fidelity.

Data Teams provide another system of support. Align your current Data Team purpose and responsibilities to ensure implementation of your system of RtI, with integrity and fidelity.

Referral Processes and Documentation

While referral for consideration of special education services is not the goal or purpose of RtI, it is a possible outcome. Students who do not show expected improvement after continued and intensive interventions – two or more interventions implemented with *integrity* and *fidelity* – should be reviewed for referral as a possible candidate for special education evaluation. For identification as a student with a disability, students must meet specific criteria outlined by IDEA and state regulations for at least one disability category and must demonstrate the need for specially designed instruction – meaning the disability must have an adverse impact on educational performance. It is equally important to note that some disability categories (i.e. Autism, Intellectual Disability, Brain Injury, Vision and Auditory Impairments, some health impairments, etc.) may warrant immediate referral for consideration of evaluation for special education services without any interaction with RtI.

IDEA 2004 encourages schools to use alternative research-based procedures for determining a student has a specific learning disability, such as a system of RtI.

According to the IDEA 2004 reauthorization, schools must also consider low achievement and inadequate response to interventions regardless of a discrepancy in achievement and ability. IDEA 2004 encourages schools to use alternative research-based procedures for determining a student has a specific learning disability, such as a system of RtI. For schools that have not moved to such a system, the data gathered are still very useful as evaluation is required in all states. Information from each prevention level will help guide the evaluation by identifying specific areas for diagnostic assessment. Additionally, use of prevention level data can be used as documentation in support of the adverse impact associated with an indentified Specific Learning Disability. Because this information is valuable to inform the eligibility determination process, it will be important for teams to ensure that data are collected with integrity and fidelity throughout RtI.

When schools can use RtI data to support the identification of a specific learning disability as well as when schools use RtI data to support adverse impact associated with a disability, some specific pieces of information need to be included.

When schools can use RtI data to support the identification of a specific learning disability as well as when schools use RtI data to support adverse impact associated with a disability, some specific pieces of information need to be included. Teams must become familiar with the documentation and procedural requirements for pre-referral and referral in their school. At the least, documentation must include the following, for each intervention implemented – with room for multiple interventions to be documented:

- Student performance prior to beginning the intervention (baseline performance).

- Performance goal with anticipated time to reach the goal (end of year performance commonly used).

- Area of risk addressed by the intervention (i.e. math computation).

- Description or name of the intervention (i.e. cover-copy-compare).

- Frequency of intervention sessions (i.e. daily).

- Duration of intervention sessions (i.e. 20 minutes).

- Dates of intervention (often represented by start and stop dates).

- Result of intervention or intervention outcome (Did the student improve? Enough?).

RtI documentation sheets can be found as examples or templates from a variety of sources and range from very simple and basic to complex and detailed. Many states, school districts, and/or schools have existing referral and documentation forms that can be revised to include necessary and desired information. In all states, inappropriate instruction must be ruled out before considering a Specific Learning Disability. Documentation of RtI with integrity and fidelity across prevention levels allows teams to demonstrate appropriate instruction has occurred.

Other RtI Related Items for Which to Plan

The above tools will help the RtI Team plan for a system of responsiveness to interventions. In addition to the details defined in these tools, the RtI Team will need to plan for the following:

- Professional learning experiences and processes.

- Enhancing primary prevention for schools with an upside down triangle.

- Resources to support RtI implementation.

- Policies, procedures, and guidelines.

- Teachers' "toolbox" for providing high quality instruction and interventions.

Applying RtI to Behavior

Although applying behavior to RtI is beyond the scope of this book, it is mentioned, when appropriate, throughout the book. PBIS Implementation Guides #24 through #33 in the *RtI Implementation Guide* are included to support those of you working on implementing a system of response to intervention for behavior.

PBIS Implementation Guides #24 through #33 in the RtI Implementation Guide are included to support those of you working on implementing a system of response to intervention for behavior.

Book Study Questions

1. Why is it important to spell out the details of all the components of your system of RtI before implementation?

2. What elements of a system of RtI are already present in your school, but may need coordination and systematizing?

3. What are the requirements for documentation prior to, and procedures to follow for, referral for consideration of evaluation in your school?

Application Opportunities

1. Use the tools in the RtI Implementation Guide to begin planning your system of RtI.

2. Use these materials to guide your study as you learn about RtI components, then commit to RtI implementation.

3. Identify key personnel who have pivotal influence in your school to inform and enlist early in the design process.

4. Identify key personnel who already embrace the concept, intent, and principles of RtI to enlist in the process.

CHAPTER 5

Build Capacity

*Check the position of your capacity gauge before tackling
any challenge as it may take more or less than you "have."*

William Maphoto

Once teams have completed the strenuous and exciting work of using the RtI Implementation Guide to develop the *Plan* for their system of RtI, it is time to *Build the Capacity* of all staff members to understand and fulfill their roles and responsibilities. This includes the challenging process of sharing the plan with all stakeholders.

Build Capacity

Building capacity means . . . *to strengthen parties' ability to work together for their mutual benefit by providing them with the skills and tools they need to define problems and issues and formulate solutions.* (Michelle Maiese in "Capacity Building.")

Building Capacity with RtI is about making sure all components of the system of RtI are understood, agreed upon, doable, and committed to by all staff members. *Building Capacity* to implement RtI includes the following:

Building Capacity with RtI is about making sure all components of the system of RtI are understood, agreed upon, doable, and committed to by all staff members.

- ◆ Helping staff understand the sense of urgency to implement the system of RtI.

- ◆ Enlisting all staff to commit to implementing the intent, purpose, and components of RtI.

- ◆ Refining roles and responsibilities of all staff members.

- ◆ Identifying where and how the structures of RtI fit and complement existing efforts, activities, and systems.

- ◆ Helping staff understand how the parts work together to create the whole.

- ◆ Establishing a system to support implementation, with integrity and fidelity.

- Establishing a system to monitor RtI processes and implementation with integrity and fidelity.

- Establishing a system to evaluate the efficiency and effectiveness of processes associated with the system of RtI.

- Communicating the details of the school's system of RtI to all stakeholders.

- Establishing a visual document of intervention expectations for each level at the school. (See RtI Implementation Guides #17 and #18.)

Leaders and Leadership Structures

Successful implementation of RtI and CSI hinges on effective leadership. We see the job of leaders as helping everyone in the organization implement the shared vision. All staff are leaders.

Organizations with strong leaders and leadership teams developed through CSI will have structures in place to manage the components and activities associated with RtI implementation.

Organizations with strong leaders and leadership teams developed through CSI will have structures in place to manage the components and activities associated with RtI implementation. School leaders ensure the vision is articulated and reinforced throughout the school. Strong leaders:

- interact with and involve all staff, providing support to ensure strong communication, flexibility, and refinement of the system, based on data.

- interact with and involve central office and district administration to share outcomes in addition to obtaining and sustaining needed resources.

- interact with and involve parents and community organizations to share processes, outcomes, and enlist support.

- listen to all levels of the organization to make and communicate decisions regarding implementation effectiveness and changes needed.

- protect and honor allocated time and resources needed for collaboration, professional learning, comprehensive data analysis, and implementing interventions across all levels of prevention.

- remain focused on the big picture of RtI's principles and promises.

- differentiate between a deficit and risk model.

- acknowledge RtI may look different at different levels of the school (i.e. early elementary with an inverted pyramid and later elementary in which the pyramid is right sided).

- model with purpose and intensity.

Leaders utilize the leadership team and structures available to design, implement, monitor, and evaluate with *integrity and fidelity.*

Sharing with Staff

As with all change, some staff will welcome the structures, resources, and supports that have been designed for implementation, while others will be more hesitant to commit and engage in the activities required. In working with schools to develop, implement, monitor, and evaluate a system of RtI, the authors have administered questionnaires to help teams learn where an entire staff stands with respect to their understanding of RtI. The results from questionnaires administered to 1,938 staff members from 76 schools have some glaring results, which have implications for building staff capacity. Staff were asked how they learned about RtI and how they wanted to learn about RtI going forward. The majority of staff members (over 55%) reported they learned about RtI through faculty meetings. Fewer than 5% responded that they would *like* to learn about RtI in a staff or faculty meeting going forward, with professional learning workshops as the preferred learning choice (37%). This is important information going forward for these schools as most of the respondents (62%) noted they could not describe the RtI components.

Failure to adequately prepare staff who will be implementing RtI processes by helping them understand the what, why, and how behind RtI decreases the commitment and opportunity for implementing the plan with *integrity and fidelity.* For this reason, the *Build Capacity* stage is often seen as the *make it or break it stage.*

Professional Learning

Staff need to fully understand the intent and purpose of the system of RtI to consistently implement with *integrity and fidelity.* Teams may need to identify specific and ongoing professional learning based on staff skills, knowledge, and readiness for implementation. Some staff will need multiple opportunities to adjust thinking, and perhaps change attitudes or beliefs about her/his role as an educator, the purpose of public education, what literature describes, and what rules, regulations, and laws guide our planning.

Staff need to understand principles which underlie the system of RtI, including:

- ◆ Differences between a deficit model and a risk model, and the resulting instructional approaches.

- ◆ RtI is a system. All grade level and content areas need to work together to ensure a continuum of learning that makes sense for *all* students.

*Leaders utilize the leadership team and structures available to design, implement, monitor, and evaluate with **integrity and fidelity.***

*The **Build Capacity** stage is often seen as the make it or break it stage.*

*Staff need to fully understand the intent and purpose of the system of RtI to implement with **integrity and fidelity.***

- RtI must be implemented with *integrity and fidelity.* Staff must implement agreed upon universal strategies for addressing learning needs and classroom management.

- The best way to implement RtI is to deliver effective, evidence-based, primary level core instruction.

- All students receive *Primary Level* instruction – always. *Secondary* and *Tertiary Prevention Levels* are additionally provided to those identified at risk through established assessments followed by procedures and processes for confirming risk status.

- Data are required to support decision making regarding intervention effectiveness.

- Use of multiple strategies must be documented, with a record of student response to each intervention, prior to referral for consideration of evaluation for special services.

To ensure understanding and implementation of all RtI components, RtI teams should plan professional learning activities to support staff acquisition of skills and knowledge, as well as to help with a shift in attitudes and beliefs.

To ensure understanding and implementation of all RtI components, RtI teams should plan professional learning activities to support staff acquisition of skills and knowledge, as well as to help with a shift in attitudes and beliefs. Implementation monitoring with tools such as Support Protocols and collaboration structures will elicit needed feedback about the system. Monitoring activities can go a long way in ensuring staff can and will implement the plan to which they have committed.

Instructional Coherence

*The need for staff to implement well organized, purposeful instruction, aligned vertically and horizontally across teacher, grade level, and subjects, known as **instructional coherence,** is critical for achieving desired outcomes.*

The need for staff to implement well-organized, purposeful instruction, aligned vertically and horizontally across teacher, grade level, and subjects, known as *instructional coherence,* is critical for achieving desired outcomes.

The key to obtaining *instructional coherence* is monitoring your plan and what you expect teachers to deliver in the classroom by:

- Reviewing fidelity checklists that accompany curriculum as part of training for implementation of curriculum.

- Identifying and ensuring evidence-based instructional practices are used in every classroom through agreements about these practices, such as meaningful differentiation, scaffolding, Universal Design for Learning (UDL), cooperative learning structures, and specific strategies to enhance learning such as building vocabulary and background knowledge or teaching 'learning how to learn,' or metacognition and executive function skills, to all students.

◆ Conducting direct, structured observations based on agreements for implementation of curriculum and instruction to capture the essence of what is (and is not) being implemented with consistency.

◆ Engaging teachers in collaboration that includes an explicit structure for discussing implementation issues about curriculum or instructional activities each teacher is expected to utilize in her/his classroom.

◆ Including communication between an interventionist at the *Secondary* and *Tertiary Levels* and the teacher at *Primary Level* to ensure strategies learned at *Secondary* and *Tertiary Levels* are transferred to *Primary Intervention.*

Reaching agreements and establishing expectations regarding curriculum and instruction, and monitoring implementation will relieve staff's continual question of, "Am I doing this right?", reduce anxiety, boost confidence, and put staff on the right track for achieving identified outcomes.

Parent Involvement

It is well established that parents play a vital role in the student's readiness to learn every day. For some students, we need to provide supplemental supports to help them be ready to learn. These may include providing breakfast each morning, in addition to lunch, as well as providing needed supplies or materials. For a few students, it may also mean engaging systems outside of the school to support the entire family unit.

For students who can access support structures outside of school, we encourage involvement in some specific and general ways. First, we need to communicate our approach for supporting *all* students' learning outcomes with our *Schoolwide Prevention System* that optimizes student learning opportunities for both those who need enrichment as well as those who struggle to meet performance standards. Once parents understand we will be utilizing our expertise and knowledge in flexible ways at school to support *every* student, we can share results from this system more meaningfully. We can also host meetings or events to provide general strategies and information directly to parents and caregivers to support student learning. Finally, we can invite parents or caregivers of individual students to attend meetings where we review or discuss progress and strategies we are employing to improve student performance, review specific results in response to those strategies, and identify specific activities parents can use at home to support their children – with continued communication regarding student responsiveness and our plan for increased achievement.

Reaching agreements and establishing expectations regarding curriculum and instruction, and monitoring implementation will relieve staff's continual question of, "Am I doing this right?", reduce anxiety, boost confidence, and put staff on the right track for achieving identified outcomes.

We need to communicate our approach for supporting all students' learning outcomes with our Schoolwide Prevention System that optimizes student learning opportunities for both those who need enrichment as well as those who struggle to meet performance standards. Once parents understand we will be utilizing our expertise and knowledge in flexible ways at school to support every student, we can share results from this system more meaningfully.

Staff who engage parent organizations early in the process of launching and implementing a schoolwide prevention system for academics, as well as behavior, find parents much more responsive when their support is desired or needed for the success of a student.

Staff who engage parent organizations early in the process of launching and implementing a schoolwide prevention system for academics, as well as behavior, find parents much more responsive when their support is desired or needed for the success of a student. Staff who wait to inform parents regarding changes in ways students may access support services often spend unnecessary time responding to requests and explanations about the structures being used. Occasionally, failure to inform parents results in a system overwhelmed with outside requests for consideration of evaluation, and complaints about an unresponsive system – when we are, in fact, creating a *more* responsive system.

Book Study Questions

1. How will leaders and leadership structures support RtI implementation?

2. What are important factors to consider when preparing information to share with staff? With parents?

3. What professional learning opportunities and activities are needed to support RtI implementation?

4. How will instructional coherence enhance RtI outcomes?

5. What should parent involvement look like within a schoolwide prevention system?

Application Opportunities

1. How will you use the RtI Implementation Guide to help with *building capacity* for implementation of RtI in your school?

2. What important steps will you take to prepare staff for implementation and for sharing the RtI Plan?

3. What leadership structures do you have or need to adopt for implementation integrity and fidelity?

4. How will you involve parents?

CHAPTER 6

Implement and Monitor

*One of the great mistakes is to judge policies and programs
by their intentions rather than their results.*

Milton Friedman

Full operation of RtI occurs when the system of RtI is embraced by staff, integrated into all classrooms with *integrity and fidelity,* and embedded within all practices. Stage 4: Implement and Monitor is where the rubber meets the road. To implement with *integrity and fidelity,* teachers need to know the steps associated with RtI. RtI occurs in a cycle with some activities occurring daily, some weekly, and some at other designated times, as outlined in Figure 6.1. These activities are further detailed in the RtI Implementation and Monitoring Timeline, described in Chapter 7.

To implement with
integrity and fidelity,
teachers need to know the steps associated with RtI.

Figure 6.1
RtI Cycle of Activities

Beginning of the year	Middle of the year	End of the year	Daily	Weekly	At least every 4 to 6 weeks
Administer universal screenings. Assign students to prevention level. Identify and monitor students "on watch."	Administer universal screenings. Assign students to prevention level, adjusting lists as data indicate. Identify and monitor students "on watch."	Administer universal screenings. Confirm risk status.	Provide high quality instruction. Provide designated interventions at each prevention level.	Progress monitor students assigned to secondary or tertiary intervention. Progress monitor any students identified for a "watch list" not receiving intervention.	Review progress monitoring data for each student to determine appropriate action for successfully increasing performance in areas of risk.

Implementing RtI throughout the year involves following these steps:

◆ *Provide high quality, evidence-based curriculum and instruction, aligned to standards and the vision, with integrity and fidelity, to every student at every grade level, in every classroom.*

◆ *Administer universal screening.*

◆ *Assign students to prevention levels.*

◆ *Provide intervention sessions and implement intervention strategies.*

◆ *Evaluate effectiveness of intervention.*

◆ *Adjust intervention strategy, intervention level, or assignment to intervention, as indicated by data.*

Implementing RtI throughout the year involves following these steps:

1. Provide high quality, evidence-based curriculum and instruction, aligned to standards and the vision, with *integrity and fidelity*, to every student at every grade level, in every classroom.

2. Administer universal screening.

    a. Academic assessments administered to all students and behavior screening processes applied to all students.

    b. Generate lists of students in need of intervention based on the identified cut point or cut score.

    c. Generate lists of students (if any) who are in need of monitoring to ensure success (near the cut point), known as a "watch list."

3. Assign students to prevention levels.

    a. All students are assigned to Primary Level Prevention. **Always.**

    b. Confirm risk for students identified through universal screening procedures.

    c. Assign students to intervention(s) to increase performance in identified areas of risk.

    d. Set performance goals for each student receiving Secondary and Tertiary Intervention.

    e. Establish expectations for instructional match and differentiation of instruction at the Primary Level Prevention to ensure all students make acceptable progress.

4. Provide intervention sessions and implement intervention strategies.

    a. In addition to Primary Level Instruction, identified students receive intervention sessions or strategies to increase performance in identified areas of risk.

    b. Progress Monitor student performance weekly as a result of interventions provided.

5. Evaluate effectiveness of intervention.

    a. Compare student actual performance, represented by the trendline, to the expected performance, represented by the goal or aimline.

    b. Confirm integrity and fidelity of implementation before adjusting intervention (includes student participation and attendance); if inadequate, aggressively monitor integrity and fidelity.

6. Adjust intervention strategy, intervention level, or assignment to intervention, as indicated by data.

    a. Substantial progress: reduce intervention time for students who have met or exceeded their goal, and whom the team believes will be successful with reduced (or no) intervention.

b. Sufficient progress: continue interventions until team determines student is ready to reduce intervention time.

c. Unacceptable progress:

   (1) Questionable progress:

      i. decide to continue for a set time and re-assess or follow the reasons for making poor progress.

   (2) Poor progress:

      i. Change intervention strategy within the same level (Secondary or Tertiary), which might include changing "who" delivers the intervention.

      ii. Add components or increase intensity of interventions, effectively changing from a Secondary to a Tertiary Intervention unless the student is already in Tertiary.

      iii. Refer for consideration of evaluation for special services if there have been multiple interventions (at least two) implemented with integrity and fidelity for the designated length of time.

Knowledge of these steps leads to greater consistency with implementation because the steps clarify when specific activities occur in the System of RtI and processes. The RtI Implementation Guide clarifies how, when, and by whom, each step will be carried out.

Instructional Design for Primary Prevention

Effective instructional practices for RtI begin with Primary Level or core instruction in the general education classroom which sets the stage for identifying students who will be in need of Secondary and Tertiary Interventions. The system of RtI should be designed so that 80% or more of students acquire the skills and knowledge needed to be proficient without additional intervention. In order to make this happen, we must ensure teachers have necessary skills, especially at schools where there are high numbers of students at risk.

Teachers need a clear understanding of effective instructional practices, especially differentiating instruction, scaffolding, and Universal Design for Learning. Many other evidenced-based approaches and strategies are extremely beneficial in the classroom, but these three are cornerstones for supporting RtI. While many teachers know and understand a variety of strategies that could be used for differentiating instruction, they often lack the skills and ability to apply these strategies in context, or to differentiate *meaningfully*. Differentiation involves adjusting content, process, products, or learning environment according to student readiness, interest, or learning

Knowledge of these steps leads to greater consistency with implementation because the steps clarify when specific activities occur in the RtI system and processes.

The RtI Implementation Guide clarifies how, when, and by whom, each step will be carried out.

Teachers need a clear understanding of effective instructional practices, especially differentiating instruction, scaffolding, and Universal Design for Learning.

*Providing structures that allow students to engage in learning at their success level can lead to learning gains at the **Primary Level** without necessitating **Secondary** or **Tertiary Interventions.***

Universal Design for Learning (UDL) is an instructional approach that is gaining importance as a means to increase access for students so learning takes hold during primary level instruction and reduces the likelihood of the need for intervention.

profile. Teachers must rely on learning data to do this meaningfully at the Primary Level of prevention. Meaningful differentiation requires using data to set leveled assignments, to group students, to scaffold instruction, and determine appropriateness of other strategies. Providing structures that allow students to engage in learning at their success level can lead to learning gains at the Primary Level without necessitating Secondary or Tertiary Interventions.

Universal Design for Learning (UDL) is an instructional approach that is gaining importance as a means to increase access for students so learning takes hold during Primary Level instruction and reduces the likelihood of the need for intervention. According to the Every Student Succeeds Act (ESSA, 2015), which replaced No Child Left Behind, UDL is a framework for planning instruction prior to students entering the classroom by using flexibility in three ways – in the ways information is presented; in the ways students respond or demonstrate knowledge; and in the ways students are engaged – while reducing barriers in instruction, curriculum, materials, or the environment associated with being a student with a disability or having limited English proficiency. ESSA encourages States to monitor school district use of UDL in assessment and instruction, and encourages the use of technology as a means to support access to instruction and curriculum for all students.

Eight effective practices have been identified by the National Technical Assistance Center on Positive Behavioral Interventions and Supports (PBIS) and utilized in many state trainings. These practices, identified through decades of research as effective classroom practices, are shown in Figure 6.2.

Figure 6.2
Eight Effective Classroom Practices

Strategies to Increase Instructional Time	Strategies to Increase Student Engagement
1. Clear classroom expectations. 2. Clear procedures and routines. 3. Encourage expected behaviors with specific positive feedback. 4. Discourage inappropriate behaviors.	5. Active supervision. 6. Provide multiple opportunities for students to respond. 7. Provide varied activity sequence and student choice. 8. Consider task difficulty.

These eight strategies are very powerful for shifting the culture of a classroom from disorder to order; from punitive to positive; or from low achieving to high performing. At the very least, staff should agree to implement and monitor these eight practices. Readers are encouraged to investigate how each of these strategies will increase instruction and student engagement by accessing PBIS resources available through the National Technical Assistance Center.

These strategies also help teachers who might feel overwhelmed with the implementation of RtI. Once RtI is fully implemented, all teachers will appreciate that the system of RtI is increasing their ability to make a difference for *every* student.

Instructional Design for Secondary and Tertiary Prevention

Schools often struggle with ways to successfully implement Strategic and Intensive Interventions. Two approaches are often used: *standard protocol* approach or *problem-solving* approach. Both use evidence-based interventions and practices to address areas of risk. There are specific reasons schools may use one over the other, or a combination of both. With a *standard protocol* approach, students identified at risk in one academic area (such as math) for secondary prevention are all provided the same, research validated interventions to improve performance. This strategy often addresses multiple subskills and must be delivered with integrity and fidelity to ensure outcomes indicated by research. *Problem-solving* approach is one many schools are familiar with and involves a team knowledgeable about both the student's area of risk and the available interventions to determine which intervention will be used with each student identified at risk. Schools with larger numbers of students in need of Secondary or Tertiary Intervention often opt for a less time consuming, but still valid, *standard protocol* approach.

When using *standard protocol* approaches, schools may have trained specialists or interventionists who provide the instructional program for Secondary or Tertiary Level Instruction. Sometimes computer-assisted learning programs are used as a *standard protocol* for Secondary Level Interventions where individual sessions with adult supervision and monitoring are held inside or outside the regular classroom. A *standard protocol* approach may also mean using supplemental programs designed for intervention that correlate with the school's core curriculum. Each student enrolled in such a program and identified for Secondary or Tertiary Level Prevention receives progress monitoring each week to ensure the approach is working. Schools often address the needs of students who do not make acceptable progress under a *standard protocol* approach by employing the *problem-solving* approach to identify alternate strategies.

*With a **standard protocol** approach, students identified at risk in one academic area (such as math) for secondary prevention are all provided the same, research validated interventions to improve performance.*

Problem-solving approach is one many schools are familiar with and involves a team knowledgeable about both the student's area of risk and the available interventions to determine which intervention will be used with each student identified at risk.

*For schools with large numbers of students identified at risk for poor learning outcomes (inverted pyramids), the **standard protocol** approach may help conserve resources.*

For schools with large numbers of students identified at risk for poor learning outcomes (inverted pyramids), the *standard protocol* approach may help conserve resources. For example, a school may project the most needed reading intervention for the most likely reading difficulties based on comprehensive data analysis. If teachers can follow a *standard approach* for common areas of risk, this reduces the need for *problem-solving* RtI teams at the Secondary Level, conserving time and resources. When using a *standard protocol* approach, RtI problem-solving meetings can be reserved to Tertiary only.

In addition, problem solving for every risk factor or each student who demonstrates this need goes against the proactive model and prevention assumptions of both RtI and CSI. If we know during the summer what the likely reading difficulties will be for fourth grade reading, we should identify and plan to address these difficulties as the year begins rather than wait for students to fall behind and then problem solve.

*Many schools are familiar with a **problem-solving** approach to designing intervention strategies as it has been a hallmark of pre-referral intervention strategies for decades.*

Many schools are familiar with a *problem-solving* approach to designing intervention strategies as it has been a hallmark of pre-referral intervention strategies for decades. Schools are familiar with the process of reviewing the learning and assessment profile of an individual student to determine appropriate interventions. RtI teams should keep in mind, as a risk model for intervention rather than a deficit model, the purpose of *problem solving* is to identify patterns in student performance and subskills needed to support future success, then to match interventions to achieve this goal. While the process may look, feel, and sound similar to what was used in a previous pre-referral model, RtI teams need to be intentional in establishing the important "risk model" concept with all team members to ensure we are not just imposing new labels on existing practices.

*When staff evaluate the system of RtI and see specific weaknesses in the core curriculum and instruction that may be creating common areas of risk for students, they can begin implementing changes at the **Primary Level** to reduce the numbers of students identified at risk.*

Schools may find it beneficial to support both approaches in assigning students to interventions, often using *standard protocol* for Secondary Level and *problem solving* for Tertiary. When staff evaluate the system of RtI and see specific weaknesses in the core curriculum and instruction that may be creating common areas of risk for students, they can begin implementing changes at the Primary Level to reduce the numbers of students identified at risk. Schools with high numbers of students at risk may have to research, investigate, and even experiment with alternate classroom structures, programs, and processes to meet the high needs of students at the Primary Level. Becoming aware of common areas of risk may happen as you implement, or may be revealed during *Stage 5: Continuously Improve.* Either way, teams should strategically address the common areas of risk identified through Primary Prevention.

For either *standard protocol* or *problem-solving* approaches, the classroom teacher is often the individual directly responsible for ensuring that students identified by the RtI team to be in need of Secondary, if not Secondary and Tertiary, Interventions receive those interventions during the school day. In fact, it is often more coherent and more effective for the student and the teacher when interventions are provided in the general education classroom by the same teacher the student has for Primary Level Core Instruction.

To do this, teachers have to structure their day using effective practices that allow students to work independently – either alone or in small groups – while the teacher works with those identified at risk. The eight effective practices outlined in Figure 6.2 are helpful for structuring a classroom to this end, as are strategies for meaningful differentiation and Universal Design for Learning. Even with good strategies, teachers may need support to structure the time allocated to them for instruction and intervention. RtI teams should have resources available to assist with these structures in the general education classroom. Figure 6.3 contains an example of daily structures for an elementary classroom, or classrooms where students have one teacher most if not all of the day. Figure 6.4 contains an example of scheduling interventions at the secondary level, or grades where students have multiple teachers, usually by content, during the day. Schools may need to be creative with scheduling, time, space, and other resources to design a system in support of student learning outcomes with adequate instructional time for interventions.

*For either **standard protocol** or **problem-solving** approaches, the classroom teacher is often the individual directly responsible for ensuring that students identified by the RtI team to be in need of **Secondary**, if not **Secondary** and **Tertiary, Interventions** receive those interventions during the school day.*

Figure 6.3
Example Elementary Classroom Daily Schedule with Intervention Groups.
Highlighted areas reflect Secondary and Tertiary Prevention Level times for reading and math.

		Teacher Schedule:				Student Schedule:
	M	**T**	**W**	**R**	**F**	**Daily**
8:00	Writing instruction and individual conferences with each student during the week.					Writing conferences and independent writing (Primary Prevention)
8:40	S-r	S-r	S-r	S-r	S-r	Morning work (independent or small group assignments) Intervention Group S-r (strategic group)
9:10	Core reading instruction begins - Whole group					Core reading (Primary Prevention)
9:30	1	2	1	2	1 one week 2 next week	Reading Centers (Primary Prevention)
9:50	3	4	4	4	3	Reading Centers (Primary Prevention)
10:10	Core reading activities - Whole group					Core reading (Primary Prevention)
10:30	Independent reading work and Group T-r: direct instruction					Seat work Intervention Group T-r (Intensive group)
10:45	Planning time					Specials (library, art, music, PE)
11:35	Restroom, lunch, recess					Restroom, lunch, recess
12:20	Core Math Curriculum (whole group)					Math (Primary Prevention)
12:50	5	6	5	6	Supervise Projects	Math Group Projects (Primary Prevention and small groups)
1:20	S-m	S-m	S-m	S-m	S-m	Student Personal Agendas and Intervention Groups
1:40	T-m	T-m	T-m	T-m	T-m	
2:00	Whole Group with differentiated lessons.					Science or Health
2:30	Whole Group with differentiated lessons.					Social Studies
3:00	All students.					Dismissal

Legend:

Strategic Intervention groups in reading: Secondary Level conducted from 8:40 to 9:10 with six students for reading; other students are doing morning work (usually seatwork).

Primary Level reading groups 1, 2, 3, and 4: Core instruction held from 9:30 to 10:10 following whole group reading instruction; students receiving intervention are mixed into these groups using flexible grouping; these are not typically ability groups.

Intensive Intervention groups in reading: Tertiary Level conducted from 10:30 to 10:45 for three students using a combination of individual conferences and small group direct instruction.

Primary Level math groups 5 and 6: Core instruction held from 12:50 to 1:20 following whole group instruction; students in math small groups of 4 to 8 for support to acquire concepts and skills from Primary Level Instruction (these groups change frequently based on classroom performance); these students are also included in math project groups.

Secondary and Tertiary Intervention groups in math: Secondary (groups of 5 to 8) and Tertiary (groups of 1 to 4) levels for math intervention delivered from 1:20 to 1:40 pm; students who do not need intervention work from a personal agenda on any content, typically chosen by teacher; time may also be used to make up missed work for Primary Level students.

Figure 6.4
Example High School Classroom Schedule with Intervention Groups

In this example, Primary and Secondary Prevention Levels are served in the general classroom with Tertiary Levels receiving support through a guided study hall in their daily schedule.

Sample Teacher Schedule for 50 minute class periods:

Day 1	Day 2	Remainder of Unit
Workshop rotation: • 10 minutes warm up or "hook" for learning. • 20 minutes whole group. • 20 minutes guided practice.	Workshop rotation: • 10 minutes warm up or review • 15 minutes guided practice. • 25 minutes independent work with supplemental instruction for select students (individual or group) to solidify primary level instruction.	Primary Prevention Level students: • work independently all class period; • assigned to small groups or work individually; • follow an assignment board or personal learning agenda to continue practice of skills or extend learning (this allows for scaffolding); • Teacher monitors and checks student progress periodically. Secondary Prevention Level students: • are assigned to small groups for specific intervention activities; • work time is initiated by the teacher followed by working alone or in groups using a personal agenda or visual directions; • Teacher supervises and monitors closely. *At the Secondary and Tertiary Levels – the teacher may provide specific direct instruction, as needed, to address areas of risk and for mastery of concepts and content; all students are exposed to and held accountable in appropriate ways for core curriculum concepts and content, however.*

Prevention and intervention groups are more difficult at the high school level due to scheduling requirements and the need for students to complete credits in specific content prior to graduating. Schools with higher numbers of students in Secondary and Tertiary Levels of Prevention often identify a designated block of time or period for the entire school to engage in these support levels with students who do not require additional support accessing higher level courses. Schools who have near the expected 20% of students in need of Secondary and Tertiary Prevention are often able to blend adequate interventions in the general classroom and maintain their preferred schedule for credit acquisition.

Data teams for RtI focus on two activities –

◆ *Review of universal screening data to assign students to Secondary and Tertiary Prevention Levels and set goals. These data will also be used in monitoring effectiveness of all levels of intervention throughout the year.*

◆ *Using a "checkpoint structure" for evaluating effectiveness of interventions and making decisions for adjusting or removing interventions and when to refer for consideration of evaluation for special education services.*

Assigning students to prevention levels for academics involves reviewing the universal screening assessment results to identify each student whose performance falls below the cut score.

Data Teams for RtI

Data teams have become a common feature in schools with a variety of models, structures, protocols, and approaches available. With CSI, teams establish the importance of analyzing multiple measures and looking where data categories intersect to provide more reliable information and potential answers regarding why we are getting the results we are getting and what we need to do to improve. Data teams for RtI focus on two activities –

1) Review of universal screening data to *assign students to Secondary and Tertiary Prevention Levels* and set goals. These data will also be used in monitoring effectiveness of all levels of intervention throughout the year.

2) Using a "checkpoint structure" for *evaluating effectiveness of interventions* and making decisions for adjusting or removing interventions and when to refer for consideration of evaluation for special education services.

Implementing RtI structures means expanding your data team responsibilities to include these two activities. Data teams should consider if there are existing processes, protocols, or meetings currently in use that can be refined to include RtI data review with members from the RtI team.

Assigning students to prevention levels for academics involves reviewing the universal screening assessment results to identify each student whose performance falls below the cut score. The RtI team generates a list for each teacher to review, and employs the agreed upon process for confirming the risk status for students. Confirming risk is a step valued by classroom teachers as there are usually students in which the universal screener either does not identify in need of intervention when they really are (false negative), or those who are identified at risk when they really are not (false positive). Once risk is confirmed, the RtI team assigns students to prevention levels and sets individual goals for performance. Confirming risk is accomplished through one of the following means:

◆ Review of classroom performance through grades, work samples, classroom assessments, or other acceptable teacher provided evidence;

◆ Conduct one or more progress monitoring probes (one assessment session) to confirm a student's score;

◆ Conduct progress monitoring probes for a few weeks without intervention to monitor risk status.

Progress monitoring is also sometimes conducted for students whom our Universal Screener places on a 'watch list.' These are students for whom we are uncertain if Primary Level Instruction alone will be sufficient to make acceptable progress. While these students often do not receive Secondary Interventions, their progress monitoring data are reviewed with other students receiving Secondary Intervention with decisions to maintain or change the prevention level considered, as needed.

Setting goals involves considering where you want student performance to be as a result of providing Secondary or Tertiary Interventions. Systems commonly used by schools for universal screening and progress monitoring often assist with this process by guiding the team through choices for student outcomes. This establishes the goal and subsequent *aimline,* generated by drawing a line from the student's current performance (baseline, prior to intervention beginning) to the desired performance, determined by –

- Identifying expected performance at the end of the year.
- Identifying expected performance at the end of intervention cycle of 9 to 15 weeks.
- Identifying desired performance at a selected date or time, based on a schedule for review of data.

Evaluating effectiveness of interventions includes making decisions regarding continuing or adjusting interventions. Teams review individual student results, typically graphs generated by web or computer-based systems, and determine next steps for each student. Schools want to have progress monitoring results reported in graph form, as shown in Figures 6.5 through 6.9, for ease in decision making. The RtI or designated team judge effectiveness of interventions based on comparison of the desired student performance demonstrated by the *aimline* and actual student performance demonstrated by the *trendline.* Figure 6.5 labels these features of the graph along with *phaseline* and *data points.* A *phaseline* is a vertical line on the graph used to indicate a change, adjustment, or significant break in the intervention cycle has occurred. A *data point* is the individual mark on a graph that represents student performance on each progress monitoring probe. Data points are used to generate the *trendline* or line of best fit among the data points, providing a trajectory of student performance which allows us to see where a student's performance will go if the intervention is continued.

Setting goals involves considering where you want student performance to be as a result of providing Secondary or Tertiary Interventions.

Evaluating effectiveness of interventions includes making decisions regarding continuing or adjusting interventions.

Data from progress monitoring contained in similar graphs will be used to make one of the following decisions from Step 6 in the RtI implementation steps:

Figure 6.5
Parts of a Progress Monitoring Graph

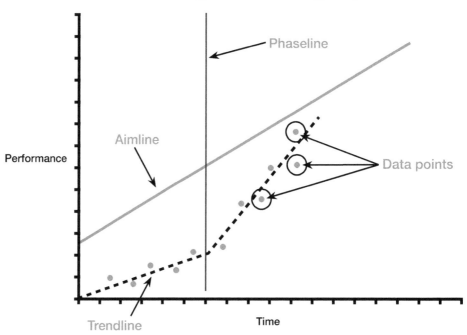

Substantial progress: For students who have met or exceeded their goal and who the team believes will be successful with reduced or no intervention, consider removal from prevention level, or reduce intervention time. See Figure 6.6 for an example graph reflecting substantial progress.

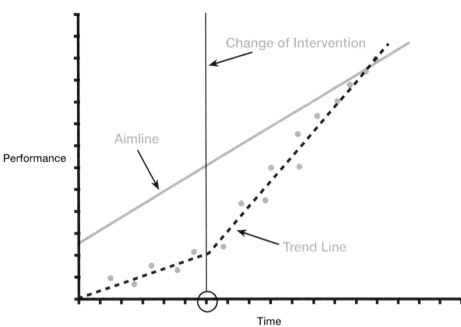

Sufficient progress: Continue interventions until team determines student is ready to reduce intervention time or be removed from prevention level. See Figure 6.7 for an example progress monitoring graph reflecting sufficient progress.

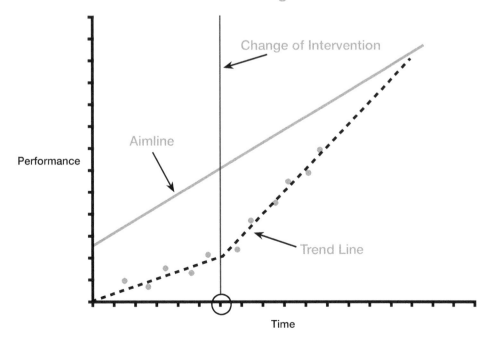

Questionable progress: Decide to continue for a set deadline to re-assess, or follow the choices for poor progress. See Figure 6.8 for an example graph reflecting questionable progress.

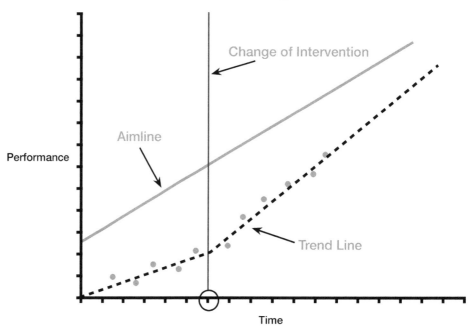

Figure 6.8
Questionable Progress

Poor progress: See Figure 6.9 for an example graph reflecting poor progress.

Options:

◆ Change intervention strategy within the same level (Secondary or Tertiary).

◆ Add components or increase intensity of interventions, effectively changing from a Secondary to a Tertiary Intervention for students not already in Tertiary.

◆ Referral for consideration of evaluation for special services if there have been multiple interventions (at least two) implemented with integrity and fidelity.

Figure 6.9
Poor Progress

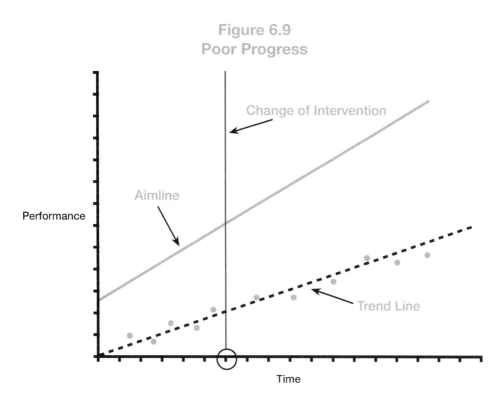

Documentation

RtI requires documentation in order to make data-informed decisions throughout the process. In the academic world, much of the documentation needed is contained in the assessment products schools use for universal screening and progress monitoring. Documentation for student responsiveness specific to Secondary and Tertiary Interventions may need to be generated for behavior, creating a format that will inform decisions regarding intervention effectiveness. Additional documentation may be needed when a referral is made for consideration of evaluation for special services. Schools often have specific referral information that must be provided in this instance. Documentation should always be a process not an event. Documenting a year's worth of Secondary and Tertiary Intervention at one time in order to process a request for consideration of referral suggest low-fidelity of implementation. Ongoing documentation of intervention suggests a thoughtful process and careful consideration throughout the RtI process. Teams should be mindful to clearly identify the intervention (automaticity, cover-copy-compare, self-instruction, etc.) not just the place interventions occurred (small group, one on one, computer assisted) to communicate implementation integrity as well.

Completed documentation forms should be maintained from one year to the next to help with monitoring students who trigger the system regularly, but often miss a needed referral due to demonstrating progress in interventions,

RtI necessitates documentation in order to make data-informed decisions throughout the process.

Documentation should always be a process not an event.

but only with the continuation of support through Secondary or Tertiary Interventions. Documentation carried from year to year can also assist with evaluating implementation outcomes in addition to helping teams and teachers begin instruction and intervention at appropriate levels each year.

Monitoring Implementation

While the activities in which your team and staff will need to engage are rather simple, monitoring implementation of curriculum, instruction, and interventions for integrity and fidelity will require dedication and perseverance. Monitoring typically includes activities from one or more of the categories described below with information regarding how to implement, and cautions for use.

Monitoring Implementation typically includes one or more of the following activities:

♦ *Direct Observation of activities in each classroom.*

♦ *Self-reporting of activities.*

♦ *Review of lesson plans and work samples.*

♦ Direct Observation of activities in each classroom, conducted by –

○ Peer observations (teacher to teacher with clear, specific feedback);

○ RtI team (may provide more consistent clear, specific feedback);

○ Specific academic or behavior coaches (may also provide more consistent clear, specific feedback);

○ Administrators.

Note: Observation activities work best when they are not used for teacher evaluation purposes. Culture of the school will often drive the ability of teachers to accept peer observations and feedback. Observation sheets with clear, specific feedback should be provided to the teacher following the observation, and not submitted elsewhere. A summary of the observation, an overall rating, or other information may be documented with no teacher name for later use in *Stage 5: Continuously Improve.*

♦ Self-reporting of activities by teachers and interventionists who are implementing identified curriculum and programs. This can occur by –

○ Having teachers complete and submit a checklist, with or without names;

○ Having teachers review established criteria during a collaborative meeting to identify what is working and what is not, or what needs more attention;

○ Peer walkthroughs with structured feedback where teachers elect to engage in activities based on self-identified needs and questions about implementation.

Since self-reporting methods are often the most unreliable, they are usually paired with other means to help maintain balance of perspective and accuracy in reporting. Self-reporting methods may be more robust for professional learning, however, so they should not be discounted.

- ◆ Review of lesson plans and work samples for indicators of coherence –

    - ○ During collaboration with multiple teachers reviewing together, involving review of only one set of lessons and work samples, sometimes anonymous and from a different grade level than the review group, with results documented in some manner (often checklists) for aggregate analysis.

    - ○ Using an established team with similar people conducting these reviews across grades periodically, documenting results, and providing feedback.

Lesson plan reviews are valuable professional learning opportunities, and it will be worthwhile for schools to consider ways for all teachers to be involved. Schools may want to have all teachers engaged in this review, paired with some self-reporting activities, to help focus the review of lessons and work samples. Incorporating peer coaching, or simply sharing challenges and supporting each other during structured collaboration times, are helpful activities.

Each category described requires a different type of resource commitment and will yield a different level of information regarding integrity and fidelity, but all will require clearly identified criteria and consistent use. One resource schools should immediately consult are the curricular materials and instructional or intervention programs used in the school. Purchased materials often include information on implementation fidelity (doing things the way they were intended). A fidelity checklist or direct observation sheet may be provided with materials. Monitoring integrity (doing things consistently) is done by scheduling one or more of the identified monitoring activities and ensuring the schedule is followed.

Book Study Questions

1. What are the implementation steps for RtI?

2. What are effective strategies that every classroom teacher should utilize?

3. Identify two approaches for providing Secondary and Tertiary Interventions.

4. Describe how a teacher can structure the day to provide the Primary Level Prevention as expected and provide Secondary and Tertiary Prevention Level supports.

5. What does the data team do in the system of RtI?

6. What are options to consider for monitoring implementation? What are the strengths and challenges for each option?

Application Opportunities

1. Complete a staff survey to inform the team regarding teacher knowledge of effective strategies including differentiating meaningfully, scaffolding, Universal Design for Learning, and the eight effective practices. Use this information to develop professional learning activities, such as peer coaching, book studies, or sharing online resources for developing skills and knowledge.

2. Apply the RtI implementation steps to your system and review them with your flowchart as a fidelity check for a comprehensively designed system.

3. Develop your data team structures to verify inclusion of appropriate structures and activities for review of RtI data, especially progress monitoring data.

4. Review the activities identified in the RtI Implementation Guide specifically for monitoring; identify individuals responsible for these activities and schedule them.

5. Monitor teams and teachers to support implementation with *integrity and fidelity,* preventing teacher burnout by obtaining feedback for creating a responsive system through surveys, team conversations, and direct observation.

CHAPTER 7

RtI Implementation and Monitoring Timeline

Planning without action is futile, action without planning is fatal.

Cornelius Fitchner

Unless commitment is made, there are only promises and hopes ... but no plans.

Peter Drucker

How long does it take to get RtI up and running? The answer is – it depends on you and your school. What do you have to do to prepare for this transformation? What structures do you have in place? What do staff understand and not understand? What do you need to do before full implementation can take place? Some schools will be able to plan and implement in a year. Others might take two or more years to do it right.

RtI Implementation and Monitoring Timeline

One thing we know for sure is that you cannot start by administering universal screeners and hope to figure out what to do along the way. It is best to think through all the processes and strategies before implementing. The RtI Implementation Guide was created to help your school think through all aspects of RtI before implementation begins. The *RtI Implementation and Monitoring Timeline* adds another lens to planning by considering RtI implementation in the context of the school year.

The *RtI Implementation and Monitoring Timeline, #19* in the RtI Implementation Guide, can help your school ensure you have planned for everything. The *Timeline* delineates what has to happen before school starts, as school starts, during the year, and at the end of the year. The form asks who is going to do this work and how its implementation will be monitored. Figure 7.1 shows the first page from the example in the RtI Implementation Guide. *PBIS* Implementation Guide #30, *PBIS Implementation and Monitoring Timeline,* does the same thing as Implementation Guide #19, for PBIS.

The RtI Implementation and Monitoring Timeline, #19 in the RtI Implementation Guide, can help your school ensure you have planned for everything.

Use PBIS Implementation Guide #30 for PBIS Implementation and Monitoring Timeline.

Figure 7.1

RtI Implementation and Monitoring Timeline

When	What	Who is going to do it?	How will you monitor this?

Before school begins	Ensure RtI components are a part of the schoolwide vision.
	
	Create an RtI Implementation Guide.
	
	Clarify special education, inclusion, pull-outs, ELL.
	
	Inform stakeholders of RtI processes and expectations.
	
	Establish roles and responsibilities.
	
	Develop expectations for instructional coherence:
	• Establish outcomes and expectations for curriculum delivery.
	• Determine common instructional approaches.
	• Agree on PBIS/PBS activities:
	  o Clarify all common procedures.
	  o Define classroom management procedures.		

	Identify research-based Universal Screening and Progress Monitoring assessments to be used in all relevant subject areas. Establish schedule for Universal Screeners (3 times per year) and Progress Monitoring Assessments (weekly). Determine all data sources that will be used to verify whether a student is at risk or not. Screening data, with two other sources of data, such as, state assessment data, classroom performance data, diagnostic assessment data, progress monitoring probe. Provide professional learning for administering Universal Screener and Progress Monitor. Inform teachers how monitoring of integrity and fidelity will occur.		

PATH Process

The *PATH Process* can put the finishing touches on your design and plan for implementing RtI.

The *PATH Process, Planning Alternative Tomorrows with Hope (PATH)*, is a planning tool, which was created by Marsha Forest, John O'Brien, and Jack Pearpoint (1994) and adapted for our purposes in implementing a system of RtI. The backward planning approach of the *PATH* process allows RtI Teams to gauge the reality of implementing their system of RtI within the timeframe identified by their goal.

The *PATH* planning tool for RtI implementation begins by having us think about the future – what do we want RtI to look like when it is fully implemented, perhaps in a year or maybe two years? Figure 7.2 shows page one of how an example middle school used the *PATH* process to plan what needs to be done to implement RtI with integrity and fidelity within one year. The entire example appears in *RtI Implementation Guide* as #20, *Our School PATH for RtI.*

The steps in the process are described below:

1. Generate the vision (what will be in place?) – The RtI Team in the example determined that they could have RtI implemented by the end of next year. In their Goal column, they described what RtI implementation will look like.

2. Describe NOW (strengths and challenges) – Staff worked during the first half of the year to study and commit to RtI. The newly assigned RtI Team worked on the RtI Implementation Guide to spell out the details of RtI. They know the RtI Team needs to put the finishing touches on the RtI Implementation Guide, bring all staff members up to date, and get RtI implemented with integrity and fidelity. Staff have many positive strengths going for them. They have several challenges as well – none of which are insurmountable, but will need to be addressed.

3. Determine action steps for implementing (backward planning) – The RtI Team determined what needed to be done 6 months from now (typically half way to the goal); 3 months; 1 month; and First Steps. Moving backward from the goal and planning each step, growing closer to where we are now, will help teams determine if their goal is attainable. This planning process allows the planners to adjust activities and the time frame as needed, to ensure all parts get done.

Use *RtI Implementation Guide #20, Our School PATH* to create your School PATH for RtI.

School PATH for RtI Steps:

- Generate the vision (what will be in place?)
- Describe NOW (strengths and challenges)
- Determine action steps for implementing (backward planning)

Figure 7.2
Our School PATH for RtI

2. Now	7. First Steps	6. One Month	5. Two Months	4. Three Months	3. Six Months	1. GOAL
Date: **DEC 2016**	Date: **JAN 2017**	Date: **FEB 2017**	Date: **APRIL 2017**	Date: **MAY 2017**	Date: **AUG 2017**	Date Created: *DEC 2016*
Strengths: ◆ All staff participated in the Comprehensive Needs Assessment process and know why RtI is needed. ◆ We have a schoolwide vision and most RtI components have been incorporated. ◆ We are clear on the purpose of RtI for our school. ◆ Our Universal Screeners have been selected. ◆ All staff have received training in the Data Team process. ◆ Some teachers have been trained and/or implementing high quality differentiated instruction strategies. ◆ Staff share data across content areas. ◆ We have an RtI Team and a Coordinator who have been intensively trained in RtI. ◆ Our RtI Team has a good start on our Implementation Guide. We need to finish it.	◆ Curriculum maps will be reviewed for all subject areas and grade levels to ensure alignment. ◆ Assessment Inventory will be adjusted to ensure no assessment overlaps, alignment to standards, and to incorporate Universal Screeners and Progress Monitors. ◆ Staff who can attend professional learning sessions on RtI will attend, and share their learning with colleagues. ◆ RtI Team will put a process in place for identifying students needing Strategic or Intensive Interventions.	◆ RtI Team works with staff, in Data Teams, to ensure all staff understand RtI components, processes, roles and responsibilities. ◆ With staff input, RtI Team completes *Our School's Response To Intervention System* Table and Flowchart for how the system of RtI will be implemented.	◆ RtI Team with staff, in Data Teams, using *Our School's Response To Intervention System* Table, to understand RtI purposes, outcomes, components, processes, roles and responsibilities.	◆ RtI Team works with staff, in Data Teams, using the RtI Flowchart and the *Our School's Response To Intervention System* Table, to understand RtI purposes, outcomes, components, processes, roles and responsibilities.	◆ Universal Screeners are administered in English Language Arts and Mathematics. ◆ RtI Team identifies the cut point for Strategic and Intensive Intervention, after reviewing all the results. ◆ Students are identified for Secondary and Tertiary Interventions using a confirmation process based on classroom performance data.	*By end of 2017-18 school year, we will have the following in place:* ◆ Staff understanding of and commitment to all aspects of RtI. ◆ Teacher understanding of effective instruction at the Primary Prevention Level. ◆ Teachers providing high quality instruction and differentiating to meet the needs of 80% of learners, 100% of the time. ◆ Instructional coherence evident throughout the school. ◆ Universal Screener implemented schoolwide in English Language Arts and Mathematics. ◆ Processes in place for identifying and confirming students in need of Secondary and Tertiary Interventions.

Book Study Questions

1. How long will it take a school to design and implement RtI?

Application Opportunities

1. Use the *RtI Implementation and Monitoring Timeline* to complete all that needs to be done by your identified time.

2. Use the *PATH* planning process to create your action plan and *PATH* to RtI implementation.

CHAPTER 8

Continuously Improve

Improving systems "prescribe adequacy but unleash greatness."

McKinsey Report

Continuous School Improvement and Evaluation

To continuously improve a system of RtI, we must evaluate the parts and the whole; make sure the parts are implemented as intended; ensure that the sum of the parts results in what we intend to be doing; and verify that the process is leading to student learning growth. We structure our RtI evaluation through the following three questions:

- Is RtI being implemented with *integrity and fidelity?*
- Is acceptable progress being made?
- What is the impact of implementing RtI?

Is RtI Being Implemented with Integrity and Fidelity?

To know if the RtI system of instruction, assessment, and interventions is being implemented as intended – with *integrity and fidelity* – we must know what was planned to be implemented, and what was implemented, while being cognizant of the original intent of RtI.

With the completed RtI Implementation Guide, it is time to go back to each component tool to ask and answer these questions:

1. Are the RtI components designed and planned consistent with their purpose?

2. Do staff members understand the components? What will you do to help them understand better?

3. Are each of the components implemented as designed, accurately and consistently?

4. What needs to improve?

5. How well do the parts work together?

We structure our RtI evaluation through the following three questions:

- Is RtI being implemented with integrity and fidelity?
- Is acceptable progress being made?
- What is the impact of implementing RtI?

In addition, Figure 8.1 shows questions to answer with data, related to *Is RtI Being Implemented with Integrity and Fidelity?* RtI Implementation Guide #21 is the entire Figure 8.1.

Figure 8.1

Is RtI Being Implemented with Integrity and Fidelity?

Evaluation Questions (Broad)	What do we want to know? (Specific)	How will we know it? (Indicator)	Where will the data come from? (Data Source and Method)	Who will capture the data? (Responsibility)	When will the evaluation occur? (Timeframe)	How will it be reported?
Is RtI being implemented with integrity and fidelity?	Is the school's RtI purpose big enough to eliminate the undesirable results found in the school needs assessment?	Analyze the needs assessment and RtI purpose.	Review *Our School's System of Response to Intervention:* #3 or #4.	RtI Team.	Before School Starts.	RtI Team to teachers.
	Is each RtI component designed and planned consistent with its purpose?	The components are spelled out in congruence with what the literature (and school) says is the purpose. Analyze the needs assessment and RtI purpose.	Review *RtI Implementation Guide.*	RtI Team.	Before School Starts.	RtI Team to teachers.
	How was RtI rolled out to staff?	Report.	RtI Team Report.	RtI Team.	As School Starts; Continuous.	RtI Team to teachers.
	Do staff members understand the components?	Staff is showing understanding in their discussions about RtI.	RtI Questionnaire; Observations; Discussions.	RtI Team.	Continuous.	RtI Team to teachers.
	Is staff committed to the implementation of RtI?	Staff is implementing with integrity and fidelity.	Number of teachers consistently implementing RtI with integrity and fidelity; RtI Questionnaire; Observations; Discussions.	RtI Team.	Continuous.	RtI Team to teachers.
	Is each component implemented as designed, accurately, and consistently?	Staff is implementing with integrity and fidelity.	Number of teachers consistently implementing RtI with integrity and fidelity; RtI Questionnaire; Observations; Discussions; *RtI Implementation Guide.*	RtI Team.	Continuous.	RtI Team to teachers.
	How can we help staff members better understand RtI and the components?	Find out what other schools do; provide each staff member with RtI Implementation Guide.	Discussions with other schools; RtI Follow-up Questionnaire; RtI Implementation Guide.	RtI Team.	Continuous.	RtI Team to teachers.
	What in the large system of RtI needs to improve?	Study evaluation results.	Evaluation Results.	RtI Team.	Continuous.	RtI Team to teachers.
	How well do the parts work together?	Study evaluation results.	Classroom and system observations; data analysis; teachers' reports.	RtI Team.	Continuous.	RtI Team to teachers.

Is Acceptable Progress Being Made?

*To know if students are making **acceptable progress,** school staff need to consider both overall progress as well as individual progress.*

To know if students are making *acceptable progress,* school staff need to consider both overall progress as well as individual progress. At the individual level, this requires staff to ask if they have moved appropriate students to the correct prevention levels for their student learning concerns, and whether they have provided them with the proper instruction and intervention. This is first informed by ongoing progress monitoring of each student while Secondary and Tertiary Interventions are provided. Knowing if there is *acceptable progress* across time requires comprehensive study of student performance on universal screening and performance assessments administered throughout the year to understand what students know and do not know.

Progress monitoring is necessary to determine if students are benefiting from instruction and intervention in ways that will lead to learning at a satisfactory rate.

Progress monitoring is necessary to determine if students are benefiting from instruction and intervention in ways that will lead to learning at a satisfactory rate, known as acceptable progress. *Acceptable progress* is determined by comparing individual student performance to the goal, typically grade level performance. This can be done with data from the *Universal Screener* as well as *Progress Monitors.* Reviewing progress monitoring data will help determine what kind of progress is being made, and if it is acceptable. See Figures 6.6 to 6.9 for descriptions of response levels that are acceptable – known as substantial or sufficient responsiveness; or unacceptable – known as poor responsiveness. Universal screening conducted three times per year identifies adequate progress or lack thereof for students receiving primary instruction without additional interventions. Universal screening data also help to understand the extent to which the achievement gap exists.

Figures 8.2 and 8.3 assist with the data review to know if *acceptable progress* is being made over time. Figure 8.2 includes evaluation questions for the universal screening data. Figure 8.3 includes evaluation questions for the progress monitoring data. RtI Implementation Guide #22 has the complete files for RtI. PBIS Implementation Guides #24 and 25 have these evaluation questions related to the PBIS Universal Screening Process, and the PBIS Progress Monitoring Process. The answer to the question, *Is RtI Being Implemented with Integrity and Fidelity?* also needs to take into consideration the results found in these two tables.

Questions to guide the evaluation of the system of interventions appear in Figures 8.4 for Primary Prevention, 8.5 for Secondary Prevention, and 8.6 for Tertiary Prevention, and in RtI Implementation Guide #23. PBIS Implementation Guides #26, #27, #28 have these file for PBIS Universal Strategies, PBIS Secondary Strategies, and PBIS Tertiary Strategies.

Figure 8.2

Is Acceptable Progress Being Made With the Universal Screener?

Evaluation Questions (Broad)	What do we want to know? (Specific)	How will we know it? (Indicator)	Where will the data come from? (Data Source and Method)	Who will capture the data? (Responsibility)	When will the evaluation occur? (Timeframe)	How will it be reported?
Is acceptable progress being made? **Universal Screeners**	Do the Universal Screeners identify students at risk of failing to meet the grade level standards?	Number and percentage of students identified as at-risk and how many students "should" have been identified, with respect to their end of year scores, by classroom, grade level, subject area, and for the school.	Universal Screener Program; State Assessments.	RtI Team, with support of teachers.	Beginning and end of year.	RtI Team to teachers.
	Do the cut points need to be adjusted?	Number and percentage of students showing learning growth on the Universal Screeners throughout the year, and compared to other assessments.	Universal Screener Program; other assessments.	RtI Team.	Each time the Universal Screener is administered.	RtI Team to teachers.
	Do students show learning growth on the Universal Screeners?	Number and percentage of students showing learning growth on the Universal Screeners from the beginning of the year to the middle of the year, from the middle of the year to the end of the year, from the beginning of the year to the end of the year.	Universal Screener Program.	RtI Team.	Each time the Universal Screener is administered.	RtI Team to teachers.
	Do Universal Screeners predict other assessment results used in the classroom?	The correlation of the Universal Screener results with other assessments.	Universal Screener Program; other assessments.	RtI Team, with support of teachers.	Each time the Universal Screener is administered.	RtI Team to teachers.
	How are teachers using Universal Screener information for Primary instruction?	Teachers report the Universal Screeners gave them valuable information to deliver quality Primary Prevention lessons.	Teacher reports.	RtI Team, with support of teachers.	Each time the Universal Screener is administered.	RtI Team to teachers.

Figure 8.3

Is Acceptable Progress Being Made With the Program Monitor?

Evaluation Questions (Broad)	What do we want to know? (Specific)	How will we know it? (Indicator)	Where will the data come from? (Data Source and Method)	Who will capture the data? (Responsibility)	When will the evaluation occur? (Timeframe)	How will it be reported?
Is acceptable progress being made? **Progress Monitors**	Do the Progress Monitors allow us to make appropriate decisions for instruction?	Number and percentage of students assigned to interventions who met or exceeded expected learning growth.	Progress Monitor Program.	RtI Team, with support of teachers.	Monthly.	RtI Team to teachers.
	Do the Progress Monitors allow us to make appropriate decisions for grouping?	Number and percentage of students who met or exceeded expected learning growth.	Progress Monitor Program.	RtI Team, with support of teachers.	Monthly.	RtI Team to teachers.
	Do the Progress Monitors help us make accurate decisions for meeting grade level standards?	Number and percentage of students doing well on Progress Monitoring compared to other performance indicators.	Progress Monitor Program; other performance indicators.	RtI Team, with support of teachers.	Monthly.	RtI Team to teachers.
	Do the Progress Monitors allow us to make accurate decisions for referring students for evaluation?	Number of students referred for evaluation from RtI and number of those who qualified.	Special Education referral data.	RtI Team, with support of teachers.	Monthly.	RtI Team to teachers.
	Do students show learning growth on the Progress Monitors, in Strategic Interventions?	Number and percentage of students in Strategic Interventions showing learning growth on the Progress Monitors.	Progress Monitor Program.	RtI Team, with support of teachers.	Monthly.	RtI Team to teachers.
	Do students show learning growth on the Progress Monitors, in Intensive Interventions?	Number and percentage of students showing learning growth in Intensive Interventions on the Progress Monitors.	Progress Monitor Program.	RtI Team, with support of teachers.	Monthly.	RtI Team to teachers.
	Do Progress Monitors correlate with other assessments used in the classroom?	The correlation of the Progress Monitor results with other assessments.	Progress Monitor Program; other assessments.	RtI Team, with support of teachers.	Monthly.	RtI Team to teachers.
	How are teachers using Progress Monitoring information to improve their instruction?	Teachers report the Progress Monitors gave them valuable information to deliver high quality lessons.	Teacher reports.	RtI Team, with support of teachers.	Monthly.	RtI Team to teachers.

Figure 8.4

Is Acceptable Progress Being Made in Primary Prevention?

Evaluation Questions (Broad)	What do we want to know? (Specific)	How will we know it? (Indicator)	Where will the data come from? (Data Source and Method)	Who will capture the data? (Responsibility)	When will the evaluation occur? (Timeframe)	How will it be reported?
Is acceptable progress being made? **Primary Prevention**	Do all classrooms show evidence of high quality instruction?	Number and percentage of students who met or exceeded expected learning growth rates.	Generate answers by review of processes: instructional coherence; by review of student learning data: # proficient and # in need of Primary Prevention only; learning growth for students in Primary Prevention only from beginning to end of year.	RtI Team, with support of teachers.	Each time an assessment is used, and at the end of grading periods.	RtI Team to teachers.
	How well do our instructional approaches and curriculum serve our students?	Does the number of students at Primary Prevention stay the same or increase from beginning to end of year (or maintain at 80% or better)? Does the number of students in need of Secondary or Tertiary Interventions decrease from the beginning to the end of year or maintain at a low level (20% or less combined in Secondary and Tertiary)?	Universal Screener data; State Achievement Tests; Formative Assessments, disaggregated by student groups.	RtI Team, with support of teachers.	Each time an assessment is used, and at the end of grading periods.	RtI Team to teachers.
	How many students do we have at or above grade level, throughout the year?	Number and percentage of students who met or exceeded grade level expectations.	Universal Screener data; State Assessment Data; Common Formative Assessments.	RtI Team, with support of teachers.	Each time an assessment is used, and at the end of grading periods.	RtI Team to teachers.

Figure 8.5
Is Acceptable Progress Being Made in Secondary Prevention?

Evaluation Questions (Broad)	What do we want to know? (Specific)	How will we know it? (Indicator)	Where will the data come from? (Data Source and Method)	Who will capture the data? (Responsibility)	When will the evaluation occur? (Timeframe)	How will it be reported?
Is acceptable progress being made? **Secondary Prevention**	How well do our Secondary strategies work for our students?	Analyze the number of students served at the strategic intervention level; length of time and number of sessions before intervention is no longer needed. Inform intervention match and effectiveness with student needs.	Number of students eligible for Secondary Prevention after each Universal Screener; number of students improving through Secondary on Progress Monitoring probes and amount improved.	RtI Team, with support of teachers.	Monthly.	RtI Team to teachers.
	How well do the Secondary curriculum materials, instruction and interventions help students reach expected levels?	Review number of students starting and ending at this level. Number and percentage of students improving through Secondary Prevention based on Progress Monitoring probes and amount improved.	Universal Screener; Progress Monitor; Common Formative Assessments.	RtI Team, with support of teachers.	Monthly.	RtI Team to teachers.
	Do we have common and frequent performance deficits in Secondary Prevention that need to be addressed in Primary Prevention?	Universal Screener data, Progress Monitoring, and other student performance data show common areas of risk.	Universal Screener; Progress Monitor; Common Formative Assessments.	RtI Team, with support of teachers.	Monthly.	RtI Team to teachers.
	Were all students in need of Secondary Prevention able to receive it? Do our cut points work for grouping our students?	Number of students eligible for Secondary Prevention after each Universal Screener remains the same or less; Do students in Primary Prevention only maintain learning growth to stay in Primary?	Universal Screener; Progress Monitor; Common Formative Assessments.	RtI Team, with support of teachers.	Monthly.	RtI Team to teachers.
	Are there students not being served in our system of RtI? How do we address this?	Review of State Assessments for students who are low performing and did not receive any or much RtI support.	Universal Screener; Progress Monitor; Common Formative Assessments.	RtI Team, with support of teachers.	Monthly.	RtI Team to teachers.
	Are we able to provide support to students above and well above grade level?	Review of processes; review of performance data.	Universal Screener; Progress Monitor; Common Formative Assessments.	RtI Team, with support of teachers.	Monthly.	RtI Team to teachers.

Figure 8.6
Is Acceptable Progress Being Made in Tertiary Prevention?

Evaluation Questions (Broad)	What do we want to know? (Specific)	How will we know it? (Indicator)	Where will the data come from? (Data Source and Method)	Who will capture the data? (Responsibility)	When will the evaluation occur? (Timeframe)	How will it be reported?
Is acceptable progress being made? **Tertiary Prevention**	How well do our Tertiary strategies work for our students?	Analyze the number of students served at the intensive intervention level; length of time and number of sessions before intervention is no longer needed. Inform intervention match and effectiveness with student needs.	Number of students eligible for Tertiary Prevention after each Universal Screener; number of students improving through Tertiary on Progress Monitoring probes and amount improved.	RtI Team, with support of teachers.	Monthly.	RtI Team to teachers.
	How well do the Tertiary curriculum materials, instruction, and interventions help students reach expected levels?	Review number of students starting and ending at this level.	Number of student improving through Tertiary Prevention based on Progress Monitoring probes and amount improved.	RtI Team, with support of teachers.	Monthly.	RtI Team to teachers.
	Do we have common and frequent performance deficits in Tertiary Levels that need to be addressed in Primary Prevention?	Review of Universal Screener data; review of Progress Monitoring and other student performance data for common areas of risk.	Review of Universal Screener data; review of Progress Monitoring and other student performance data for common areas of risk.	RtI Team, with support of teachers.	Monthly.	RtI Team to teachers.
	Were all students in need of Intensive Intervention able to receive it? Do our cut scores work for grouping our students?	Number of students eligible for Tertiary Prevention after each Universal Screener remains the same or less; Do students in Primary Prevention only maintain learning growth to stay in Primary?	Review of Universal Screener data; review of Progress Monitoring and other student performance data for common areas of risk.	RtI Team, with support of teachers.	Monthly.	RtI Team to teachers.
	Are there students not being served in our system of RtI? How do we address this?	Review of processes; review of performance data.	Review of processes; review of performance data.	RtI Team, with support of teachers.	Monthly.	RtI Team to teachers.

What Is the Impact of RtI Implementation?

To determine the impact of implementing RtI, one must consider the intended outcomes of RtI, as the system is designed. From your work earlier in this book and in your RtI Implementation Guide, your RtI Team and staff have spelled out the answers to three important questions:

- *What is the purpose of your system of RtI?*
- *What are the outcomes?*
- *Is your system of RtI "big enough" to eliminate the needs uncovered in your needs assessment?*

Gather data to answer the questions implied in the outcomes. Incorporate the information discovered in the other two major evaluation questions, and you will be able to determine the impact of your school's RtI implementation.

Gather data to answer the questions implied in the outcomes. Incorporate the information discovered in the other two major evaluation questions, and you will be able to determine the impact of your school's RtI implementation. These results will appear in the last column of Implementation Guide #2: *Our School's System of Response to Intervention.*

Book Study Questions

1. What components of RtI need to be evaluated?

2. How can you know if there is integrity and fidelity of RtI implementation?

3. How can you know if acceptable progress is being made with an RtI system?

4. How can you know the impact of RtI implementation?

Application Opportunities

1. Develop an evaluation plan for your programs and processes, including RtI.

2. Determine how you will know if acceptable progress is being made in your school's system of RtI.

3. Determine how you will know if there is integrity and fidelity of RtI implementation in your school's system of RtI.

4. Determine how you will know the impact of your school's RtI implementation.

CHAPTER 9

Summary and Conclusions

RtI is a dramatic redesign of general and special education; both need to change and the entire system needs reform.... Tweaking will not be sufficient.

The National Association of State Directors of Special Education (NASDSE)

As a guidebook, *Response to Intervention (RtI) and Continuous School Improvement (CSI): How to Design, Implement, Monitor, and Evaluate a Schoolwide Prevention System,* (2nd ed.). provides comprehensive details about how to design, implement, monitor, and evaluate a high quality schoolwide prevention system through the various stages of implementation.

Starting with continuous school improvement – reviewing the school's data, getting all staff believing that every student can learn, agreeing on a shared vision, getting communication and collaboration structures in place to implement the vision – is the best way to rethink how student needs are being met, and to accelerate the change required to ensure *every* student's learning growth, every year. Incremental change is simply not enough to meet the needs of *every* student.

The next best thing schools can do to prepare for RtI is to review the core curriculum and instruction. Is it implemented with integrity and fidelity to achieve instructional coherence? Is each classroom a high quality classroom? If the answer to either question is no, stop here, and make these yes before proceeding.

Take a look at your data teams. Do your data teams really know how to review achievement data and use these data to help teachers target their instruction to meet the needs of students? Do they understand what the indicators in the Universal Screener are assessing and what risk factor is targeted? Do teams and teachers know what is being monitored in the

As a guidebook, Response to Intervention (RtI) and Continuous School Improvement (CSI): How to Design, Implement, Monitor, and Evaluate a Schoolwide Prevention System, (2nd ed.), provides comprehensive details about how to design, implement, monitor, and evaluate a high quality schoolwide prevention system through the various stages of implementation.

Progress Monitor and how to translate student performance into changes of instruction? Do your data teams know how to focus on the bigger picture, rather than just one standard at a time? If the answer to any of these question is no, you must make this improvement before proceeding.

Stages of Implementation

To implement the purpose and intent of Response to Intervention as described and exemplified in this book, all staff members must shift their thinking and practices. To truly transform a school to implement RtI with integrity and fidelity, staff members need to embrace components of the five Stages of Implementation:

To implement the purpose and intent of Response to Intervention as described and exemplified in this book, all staff members must shift their thinking and practices. To truly transform a school to implement RtI with integrity and fidelity, staff members need to embrace components of the five Stages of Implementation.

Stage 1: Study and Commit

- ◆ Truly believe that *every* student can learn.
- ◆ Take a comprehensive and honest look at all data to understand where the school is as an organization, and how the organization is doing with respect to ensuring that every student is learning.
- ◆ Understand how the school is getting its current results to know which processes need to improve, which processes need to be kept, and which processes need to be eliminated to get different results.
- ◆ Read best practices and engage in professional learning about RtI and how to meet the needs of *every* student.
- ◆ Believe in and understand the mission of the school. A shared vision, based on the core values and beliefs of the staff, describes what it will look like when the mission of the school is being carried out by all staff.
- ◆ Complete a school improvement plan to implement the vision and put the RtI specifics into motion.
- ◆ Agree on the purpose of RtI for the school.
- ◆ Ensure all staff commit to putting the system of RtI in place.

Stage 2: Plan

- ◆ After agreeing and committing to RtI, planning begins. Specific details of RtI components, e.g., universal screeners, progress monitors, levels of prevention, data team processes, and more will need to be defined.
- ◆ Roles and responsibilities must be spelled out so everyone understands them in the same way, and so the entire system can undergo dramatic change.
- ◆ Policies, procedures, guidelines, and reallocation of resources to support RtI implementation need to be reviewed and updated.

Stage 3: Build Capacity

- Leaders must become knowledgeable of RtI and be able to translate the intent into action. They must become master collaborators, observers, and interveners.

- Teachers must become knowledgeable of RtI and able to translate the purpose of RtI into action. They must also become leaders, collaborators, data analysts, assessors, and managers of the instructional environment.

- A description and flowchart of the RtI system will help lay out the parts and show how the parts work together to create the whole. This is important so every teacher can see what is expected of her/him.

- Leadership must ensure that structures are in place to support the system and to assist teachers with the implementation of strategies to help struggling learners.

- Collaborative teams must be formed to review student learning data to carry out the intent and components of RtI.

- Schoolwide professional learning, book studies, shared readings, peer coaching, demonstration lessons, and shared experiences within the school day help all staff members learn how to meet the needs of students, and to assist with the implementation of RtI.

Stages of Implementation:

- *Stage 1:* Study and Commit
- *Stage 2:* Plan
- *Stage 3:* Build Capacity
- *Stage 4:* Implement and Monitor
- *Stage 5:* Continuously Improve

Stage 4: Implement and Monitor

- A calendar with collaborative and RtI team meeting dates, and what the teams should be discussing at that time, will help implement RtI, and keep the flow of the work continuing as planned.

- Classroom observation tools should include elements of the vision and the system of RtI to assist teachers in implementing the vision, and in knowing what RtI should look like in their classrooms.

- Classroom observation tools that focus on monitoring integrity and fidelity will assist in providing feedback to teachers and support evaluation of the system.

- Having classroom data accessible and easy to understand are a must for helping teachers know which students are responding to specific interventions.

- Parents have unique insights about their child's strengths and challenges and are frequently eager to help with interventions at home. Parents need continuous updates on their child's progress, and they need to know how they can support their child's learning so they can be true partners in the teaching/learning process.

Communicate effectively with parents regarding assessment and progress monitoring results and help parents identify ways to foster a love of learning in their children.

Stage 5: Continuously Improve

- The parts and the alignment of the parts that create the whole of the RtI system need to be monitored and evaluated on an ongoing basis. This work helps staff know they are on the right track, what needs to change to improve results, and adds accountability to the entire process.

- In order to refine the prevention system, the integrity and fidelity of implementation must be assessed; acceptable progress must be determined; and the impact of RtI implementation must be verified.

Response to Intervention (RtI) is a comprehensive delivery system in which teachers use researched-based instructional strategies and assessments to meet the needs of every student.

What RtI is Not

While the authors have written in terms of what to do to successfully design and implement RtI, we want to make clear that some of the ways we are seeing RtI implemented is not the way RtI is intended to be implemented. Response to Intervention (RtI) is a comprehensive delivery system in which teachers use researched-based instructional strategies and assessments to meet the needs of every student. RtI is not:

- A pre-referral system for special education, alone.

- A system that prevents the timely identification of special education.

- Sending the bottom 20% of students to an RtI period.

- Pulling out the "bubble students" to push them to proficiency.

- Pull-outs, alone.

- Adding after-school programs to do interventions.

- Hiring an RtI teacher.

- Buying an intervention program.

- Securing an intervention room.

- Starting or ending the day with a 45-minute intervention class, with students grouped by abilities.

Many teachers, schools, and entire districts struggle with the design, implementation, and evaluation of their schoolwide prevention systems. We are often surprised at how quickly faculty or team meetings turn to the identification of students with learning disabilities as part of designing their system of RtI. While RtI must be sensitive to this need in order to best serve every student, it is not the true purpose and intent of RtI. It is merely one outcome for a small percentage of students when the RtI system is implemented correctly.

Perhaps the word "intervention" is getting in the way. Or perhaps it is that some staffs do not have a vision (no big picture) that clarifies how they can measure and meet the needs of every student. Perhaps they have not made a true shift from a deficit model to a risk model.

As schools redesign regular and special education together to implement robust systems of RtI, some unforeseen changes may occur. One of the best-anticipated changes is that there should be fewer students identified for special services, and those who are identified will be students who will benefit most from special services. Following are some of the unexpected changes that could happen as your school reinvents itself. These may be unpleasant, but they do not mean stop.

- Some teachers will not like the idea that someone is forcing them to work differently. This could lead to teachers becoming uncooperative, or even leaving the job. Keep going – RtI will provide better learning for students, and what teacher does not want that?

- For other teachers who may not like the idea that someone is forcing them to work differently, listen carefully and ask questions. Often it is a veteran teacher who says "been there, done that." They may be loud, but they also may not be saying they will not do it. They need to know that the new way of doing business is going to last, and that it will benefit students.

- Some specialists, like school psychologists, counselors, and special educators, may not like the idea that someone is forcing them to work differently. Because they are often employees of the school district, and not the school, it becomes difficult to implement a schoolwide system of RtI with integrity and fidelity when the district might not be "there" yet. Sometimes schools have to work around these individuals if the district level supervisors are not willing to understand and support the true implementation of RtI.

- Some teachers may try to pressure school staff to stop the system of RtI because they do not want to work so hard. Hopefully, the teachers who believe in the intent and result of RtI to reach every student and prevent failure will get the others back on track. If the teachers who realize the value of RtI do not speak up, the principal must.

◆ Even though staff might be working extremely hard to implement the components of RtI as agreed upon, student achievement scores could go down at first. That is when a strong and exhaustive evaluation that helps staff understand the impact of their actions needs to take place. It could be the assessment system was not comprehensive enough or aligned to the standards being assessed, and/or the interventions were not implemented with fidelity. It could also be an indicator that teachers need to learn more about the students they have in their classrooms and look closely at the processes they are using to implement the strategies they are delivering.

◆ Even though the whole system of RtI is spelled out, some staff may focus most of their efforts on the lowest achieving students to the detriment of the higher achieving students. Every school implementing a multi-level prevention system needs to make sure the Primary Level of instruction is robust and provides quality instruction for the students who are already proficient, as well as the ones they want to get to proficiency.

◆ As new concepts are identified, clarified, and implemented, "we need better communication from the Principal" may be heard throughout the school – often to the dismay of the school leader. Take that as a call for help and feedback – that teachers want to get the system right in the classrooms, they want help in knowing what it should look like in their classrooms. Sometimes, they want to know if they really have to do this. An effective RtI Team should be able to take care of this issue, almost completely.

◆ Teachers will cry for more time. RtI will take more time. Time must be adjusted to allow for new professional learning, to implement interventions, and to collaborate. It will be extremely hard, if not impossible, to implement RtI if teachers are confined to an 8 to 2:30 day. Might need to find some more time.

Everyone needs to remember that RtI will improve teaching and learning for everyone.

General and special education teachers/specialists need to be patient and flexible as they include each other as collaborators and partners in learning new strategies. A strong system of RtI requires that roles change. Everyone needs to remember that RtI will improve teaching and learning for everyone. When the school staff do the right things for students, they will see differences in student and teacher attitudes, expectations, and results.

Recommendations

As you begin to design and implement RtI, start with a comprehensive needs assessment and schoolwide vision, and keep the vision at the center of everything that you do. Do the right thing for the benefit of every child – in every classroom, in every building, in every school in the district.

Be clear so every staff member understands all the components of RtI, and what the components will look like when fully implemented. Put multiple implementation structures in place to help every teacher implement RtI with integrity and fidelity.

Use the RtI Implementation Guide to design your system of RtI. These files will automatically set you up for monitoring and evaluation.

Leaders: Only let go long enough to get a better grip. What others have described as an implementation dip is sometimes leadership backing off because the going gets tough with the implementation of RtI. When the going gets tough, model the way with intensity, and encourage the hearts of those who are involved in implementing new processes to ensure student success. Leaders must remember teachers will truly be happy when they see how their efforts significantly impact students' learning; for which there is no easy shortcut. Sometimes the implementation dip during the implementation of RtI is related to teachers' need for more knowledge of RtI – specifically, what it should look like in "my" classroom. Flowcharts, clarified intentions, peer coaching, demonstration lessons, and classroom visits are sometimes all necessary to help teachers implement RtI with integrity and fidelity.

Recovering from a "dip," or decrease in performance, requires vigilant efforts. Teachers and administrators must recognize the hard work that produces desired results and inspire each other to continue to engage in honest reflection and evaluation that will allow the school to continuously improve.

While RtI involves extremely hard work and may be difficult to implement, teachers will find renewed confidence in their abilities to make a difference in every student's learning when they are working in a school in which RtI is the way business is done. The results are definitely worth the efforts.

We wish you much success in your journey. Feel free to contact us with your questions and comments.

*Use the **Implementation Guide** to design your system of RtI. These files will automatically set you up for monitoring and evaluation.*

While RtI involves extremely hard work and may be difficult to implement, teachers will find renewed confidence in their abilities to make a difference in every student's learning when they are working in a school in which RtI is the way business is done. The results are definitely worth the efforts.

Book Study Questions

1. If you are doing CSI right, how does it lead you to the development of a system of RtI?

2. If you are doing RtI right, how does it move you to CSI?

Application Opportunities

1. What are the anticipated and unanticipated changes you are seeing as you implement RtI?

GLOSSARY

Acceleration – Refers to a wide variety of educational and instructional strategies that educators use to advance the learning progress of students who are struggling academically.

Acceptable Progress – Learning at a satisfactory rate, often demonstrated by comparing the trendline to the aimline in a progress monitoring graph for RtI.

Accommodations – Changes to instruction or assessment administration that are designed to increase students' access to materials or enable them to demonstrate what they know by mitigating the impact of a disability. They are also designed to provide equity, not advantage, for students with disabilities or learning differences. Accommodations allow students to access curriculum, materials, assessments, etc., without fundamentally altering or lowering the standards or expectations.

Aimline – Also known as the *goal line;* represents the target rate of student progress over time. The *aimline* is constructed by connecting the data points representing the student's initial performance level (base line) and the data point corresponding to the student's year-end goal or desired performance level. The *aimline* should be compared to the *trendline* to help inform responsiveness to interventions and to customize a student's instructional program.

Alternative Assessment – Used to evaluate the performance of students who are unable to participate in regular statewide achievement tests, even with accommodations. Student performance is measured based on alternate achievement standards, often focused on a functional or life skills curriculum. Alternative assessments often use performance-based items rather than traditional 'paper-pencil' or short answer tests to capture a more holistic picture of students' abilities.

Area of Concern – Educationally relevant domain in which an individual's performance is inappropriate, is unacceptable, or negatively influences educational performance.

Assessment Inventory – A listing of the various types of assessment instruments used by a district, school, or individual teachers, that includes the purpose, type, and time frame for administration.

At Risk for Poor Learning Outcomes – Students whose initial performance level or characteristics indicate poor learning outcomes unless intervention occurs to accelerate knowledge, skill, or ability development.

Baseline – A measure of performance prior to intervention. These initial data are used to establish the *aimline* and to monitor changes or improvement in individual performance.

Behavior Intervention Plan (BIP) – A plan to address problem behavior that includes, as appropriate, positive behavioral interventions, strategies, and supports; program accommodations or modifications; and supplementary aids and services that may be required to address the problem behavior.

Benchmark – Checkpoints that are tied to designated grade; skill levels at which students' progress toward mastery of a standard is measured.

Child with a Disability – Under IDEA, a child with a disability is a child evaluated as having one of the identified disabilities, and who, by reason thereof, needs special education and related services. Under Section 504, a child with a disability is a child with a physical or mental impairment that substantially limits a major life activity.

Collaboration – A systematic process of cooperation among two or more people with shared goals and perceived outcomes occurring in a climate of trust.

Collaborative team – A group of two or more people (as described above) who meet on a scheduled or as-needed basis and fill a specific function or purpose. Collaborative teams can be formed both at the district and school levels. School-based teams are developed and sustained as determined by need and are accessible to any administrator or teacher concerned with the educational needs of students.

Commit – To dedicate oneself to a belief, an activity, or a cause, and engaging in practices to ensure success.

Continuous School Improvement – The process of continuously improving the parts of an organization, and how the parts fit together to create the whole.

Coordinated Early Intervening Service (CEIS) – CEIS is a set of coordinated services for students in Kindergarten through Grade 12 who are not currently identified as needing special education or related services but who need additional academic and behavioral support to succeed in a general education environment. The 2004 reauthorization of the Individuals with Disabilities Education Act (IDEA 2004) includes a provision that allows local education agencies (LEAs) to use up to 15% of their IDEA Part B funds for CEIS. If an LEA chooses to use CEIS funds for services to children who need academic and behavioral support, it must ensure that the CEIS funds are used for one or more of the following three purposes: (1) professional development for teachers and other school staff to enable personnel to deliver scientifically based academic and behavioral interventions; (2) direct interventions, such as education and behavioral evaluations, services, and supports; and (3) offer services aligned with activities funded under the Elementary and Secondary Education Act. [§613(f) of IDEA; 34 CFR §300.226(a) and §300.226(b)].

Core Curriculum – The materials and instructional standards required of all students in the general education setting; may be instituted by local school boards, departments of education, or other agencies charged with overseeing education.

Criterion-Referenced Assessment – Criterion-referenced assessment measures what a student understands, knows, or can accomplish in relation to a specific performance objective. It is typically used to identify a student's specific strengths and weaknesses in relation to an age or grade level standard. It does not compare students to other students.

Curriculum-Based Assessment (CBA) – CBA is a broader term than Curriculum-Based Measurement (CBM). CBA has three requirements: (1) measurement materials are aligned with the school's curriculum; (2) measurement occurs frequently; and (3) assessment information is used to formulate instructional decisions.

Curriculum-Based Measurement (CBM) – CBM is an approach to measurement that is used to screen students or to monitor student progress in mathematics, reading, writing, and spelling. With CBM, teachers and schools can assess individual responsiveness to instruction. When a student proves unresponsive to the instructional program, CBM signals the teacher/school to revise that program. CBM is a distinctive form of CBA because of two additional properties: (1) Each CBM test is an alternate form of equivalent difficulty, and (2) CBM is standardized, with its reliability and validity well documented.

Cut Point – A score on the scale of a screening tool or a progress monitoring tool. For universal screeners, educators use the cut point to determine whether to provide additional intervention. For progress monitoring tools, educators use the cut point to determine whether the student has demonstrated adequate response, whether to make an instructional change, and whether to move the student to more or less intensive services.

Data-Informed Decision Making – The ongoing process of analyzing and evaluating student data to inform educational decisions including, but not limited to, approaches to instruction, intervention, allocation of resources, policy development, movement within a multi-level system, and disability identification.

Data Point – One score represented on a graph or chart, often by a dot that corresponds to a specific performance at a specific time; usually reflects each progress monitoring probe administered.

Deficit Model – Perception of weaknesses and inabilities to define educational difficulties that are believed to be intrinsic to or within the child. As a result, the child is considered less capable of learning than her or his peers. A "fix what is broken" mentality.

Diagnostic Assessment – A type of assessment which examines what a student knows and can do prior to a learning program being implemented. Allows the teacher to identify more specifically where to begin instruction for optimal learning to occur.

Differentiated Instruction – Strategies for adjusting curriculum, teaching environments, and instructional practices to align instruction with the goal of meeting the needs of individual students. Four elements of the curriculum may be differentiated: content, process, products, and learning environment. These elements may be differentiated around student readiness, interest, or learning profile.

Direct Instruction – Instructional approaches that are structured, sequenced, and led by teachers; the use of straightforward, explicit teaching techniques. Direct Instruction may be expressed in intervention programs by creating a script for staff to follow in providing instruction and corrective feedback.

Disability – An impairment of mental or physical health or a condition that creates a skills deficit, a functional limitation, or a pattern of behavior that adversely affects educational performance. A disability 1) results in educational performance that is significantly and consistently different, diminished, or inappropriate when compared to the expectations for peers, and 2) significantly interferes with the following:

   a) access to general education settings and opportunities;

b) developmental progress;

c) involvement and progress in the general curriculum; or

d) interpersonal relationships or personal adjustment.

Discrepant/Discrepancy – The comparison of an individual's performance at a point in time to established standards or the performance of peers at that same point in time.

Disproportionality – The over or under representation of racially, culturally, ethnically, or linguistically diverse groups of students in special education, restrictive leaning environments, or school disciplinary actions, compared to other groups.

Due Process – Intended to ensure students with disabilities receive a free, appropriate public education; (FAPE); outlines requirements for parents/guardians to be involved and informed; a specific set of procedures where parents may request a due process hearing if they disagree with the program recommendations of a school district. According to IDEA, two methods may be used for resolving due process disputes –mediation or a fair hearing.

Eligibility – An individual, who by nature of her or his disability and need, requires special education and related services in order to receive an appropriate education.

Emerging Practice – Includes practices that are not based on research or theory and on which original data have not been collected, but for which anecdotal evidence and professional wisdom exists. These include practices that practitioners have tried and found effective, as well as new practices or programs that have not yet been researched. Individual student data should be used to confirm effectiveness for continued use of emerging practices.

Evaluation – A systematic determination using a variety of assessment tools and strategies to gather relevant information on a child to inform decision making for eligibility.

ESSA – Every Student Succeeds Act (Public Law 114-95), signed in December 2015, is a revision to the previous No Child Left Behind Act (2002) and reauthorization of the Elementary and Secondary Education Act (1965) that outlines requirements for education nationwide with a focus on fully preparing students for success in college and career.

Evidence-based – Evidence-based practices are educational practices and instructional strategies that are supported by scientific research studies using procedures such as experimental studies, single-case studies, or strong quasi-experimental studies.

Explicit instruction – Instruction that is clear, overt, and visible.

Fidelity of Implementation – Refers to the accurate and consistent delivery of instruction or assessment in the manner in which it was designed or prescribed according to research findings and/or developers' specifications. Five common aspects of fidelity are adherence, exposure, program differentiation, student responsiveness, and quality of delivery. *Fidelity* is implementing instruction the way it is intended to be implemented.

Focused Acts of Improvement – Refers to everyone in an organization acting in congruence with the organization's shared vision.

Formative Assessment – Regular assessment of student progress which provides ongoing feedback to the student and the teacher regarding successes and failures in the learning process. Formative assessment can be formal or informal and is not necessarily used for grading purposes. Formative assessments are used to inform instruction and keep students on track for reaching expected learning outcomes.

Free, Appropriate Public Education (FAPE) – Guaranteed right of children with disabilities to receive an education that meets their special and unique needs without additional cost to the parents.

Functional Behavior Assessment (FBA) – In the school setting, functional behavior assessments (FBA) are conducted when a student exhibits serious and/or chronic challenging behavior. A basic assumption of FBA is that the student's behavior serves a purpose (i.e., it is performed to obtain a desired outcome or goal). The hallmark of an FBA is that the process involves the identification of the environmental events that predict and maintain the student's problem behavior in order to alter those variables (i.e., change or eliminate events that trigger or follow problem behavior) and promote more adaptive and acceptable skills that allow the student to appropriately access desired outcomes.

Goal Line – also known as *aimline;* The line on a graph that connects the intersection of the student's initial performance level and date of that initial performance level to the intersection of the student's expected performance at the end of the intervention (often year-end) and the date of that expected performance. It represents the expected rate of student progress over time.

Implementation – Putting a plan, process, or program into effect.

Inclusion – A service delivery model in which students with identified disabilities are educated in the general education setting with their age-group or grade level peers. Although often used interchangeably, inclusion is not synonymous with the term *least restrictive environment.* It also is not synonymous with access to the general education curriculum, or with FAPE (free, appropriate public education).

Indicators – realistic and measurable criteria of project progress. Indicators should be defined before the project starts, and allow us to monitor or evaluate whether a project does what it said it would do. In project planning; indicators form the link between theory and practice. Indicators are either quantitative or qualitative.

Individualized Education Plan (IEP) – Written, legal document that states the goals, objectives, and services for students receiving special education.

Individuals with Disabilities Education Improvement Act (IDEIA or IDEA) – Originally passed in 1975 as the Education for All Handicapped Children Act, with the latest reauthorization in 2004. It is the federal special education law that guarantees a free, appropriate public education in the *least restrictive environment* for students with disabilities from birth through age 21. IDEA 2004 allows *Response to Intervention* to be used as a basis for decision-making when determining whether a student is eligible for special education services as a student with a specific learning disability. (*Improvement* has been added by an Act of Congress.)

Instructional Coherence – Refers to instruction that is well organized and purposefully designed to facilitate learning; aligned vertically and horizontally across teachers, grade levels, courses, and/or subjects.

Insufficient Progress – Expected rate of improvement in student performance is not enough to attain or sustain proficiency as determined by comparing *trendline* performance to the goal or *aimline.*

Integrity – Implementing instruction or a program with accuracy and consistency.

Intensive Intervention – Designed to address severe and persistent learning or behavior difficulties. It also is used for students who have proven nonresponsive to secondary intervention. Intensive interventions are characterized by increased intensity (e.g., smaller group, increased time) of academic or behavioral intervention. Intensive intervention is sometimes synonymous with interventions delivered within the *Tertiary Prevention level.*

Intervention Adaptation – Teachers use data (including progress monitoring and diagnostic data) to revise, intensify, or individualize an intervention to target a student's specific needs. Strategies for intensifying an intervention may occur along several dimensions—including but not limited to changes to group size, frequency, or duration; or changes to the instructional principles incorporated within the intervention, or in providing feedback.

Intervention Session – Designated times, location, and activities for providing Secondary and Tertiary Prevention levels to students identified in need of support; always occurs in addition to Primary Prevention.

Learning Disability – The IDEA 2004 definition of a Learning Disability/Specific Learning Disability is: The child does not achieve adequately for the child's age or to meet State-approved grade level standards in one or more of the following areas, when provided with learning experiences and instruction appropriate for the child's age or State-approved grade level standards:

- (i) Oral expression
- (ii) Listening comprehension
- (iii) Written expression
- (iv) Basic reading skill
- (v) Reading fluency skills
- (vi) Reading comprehension
- (vii) Mathematics calculation
- (viii) Mathematics problem solving

Leadership Team – A group of teachers, administrators, and other staff members who serve as a governance committee. Their job is to help everyone in the school implement the shared vision, and to ensure that all Initiatives help achieve the shared vision.

Learning Trajectory – The intended path for student learning over time, based on learning objectives, learning progressions, or specified outcomes; often represented by an aim line on a graph.

Least Restrictive Environment (LRE) – As defined in IDEA 2004, the *least restrictive environment* indicates that to the maximum extent appropriate, students with disabilities (including students in public or private institutions or other care facilities) are educated with students who are not disabled; special classes, separate schooling, or other removal of students with disabilities from the regular educational environment occur only when the nature or severity of the disability of a child is such that education in regular classes with the use of supplementary aids and services cannot be achieved satisfactorily [34 CFR 612(a)(5)].

Mainstreaming – The integration of children with disabilities into a regular classroom or a nonacademic setting (music, lunch) for part of a school day.

Modifications – Changes in course content, teaching strategies, standards, test presentation, location, timing, scheduling, expectations, student responses, environmental structuring, and/or other attributes which provide access for a student with a disability to participate in a course/ standard/test, which DO fundamentally alter or lower the standard or expectation.

Monitoring – To observe and check routinely and systematically in order to gather information about the implementation of programs and processes. Information is used for evaluation and for establishing, maintaining, and sustaining integrity and fidelity.

Multi-level Prevention System – Includes three levels of intensity or prevention. The Primary Prevention level includes high quality core instruction. The secondary level includes evidence-based intervention(s) of moderate intensity. The Tertiary Prevention level includes intervention(s) of increased intensity for students who show minimal response to Secondary Prevention or who demonstrate performance significantly below expected benchmarks. At all levels, attention should be on fidelity of implementation, with consideration for cultural and linguistic responsiveness and recognition of student strengths.

Multi-Tier System of Support – A *comprehensive* system that is inclusive of all levels or tiers of academic, social/emotional, and behavioral supports provided within a school.

Norm-Referenced Assessment – Compares a student's performance to that of an appropriate peer group, often characterizing performance by a ranking such as percentile scores.

Phaseline – A vertical line drawn between data points on a performance/progress monitoring graph to indicate a change in interventions has occurred. Phase lines indicate changes in intensity, approach, specific strategy, etc. and allow for easy identification of how many interventions a student has experienced.

Positive Behavioral Intervention Support (PBIS) – A multi-level behavior support framework for enhancing the adoption and implementation of a continuum of evidence-based interventions and practices to achieve behaviorally important outcomes for all students. PBIS is a research supported system of responsiveness to interventions (RtI) for behavior that provides a decision-making framework to guide the selection, integration, and implementation of preventive and instructive practices.

Pre-referral – The purpose of the pre-referral process is to ensure that a child is provided reasonable accommodations before she/he is referred for special education assessment. Sometimes, a change in the classroom can turn performance around and make it unnecessary to consider special education services. Using strategies that draw on a child's strengths and meet her/his educational needs may be all it takes to put the child back on the road to academic and/or behavioral progress. The pre-referral team goes by different names in different places. In some schools, it's called the Student Study Team (SST), while in others, it is the Student Intervention Team, Child Study Team, Teacher Support Team, Student Assistance Team, or Student Success Team. Regardless of its name, the purpose of the team is to:

◆ work together to identify a child's educational strengths and needs,

◆ put strategies into action, and

◆ evaluate their impact so a child can succeed in the general education classroom, and

◆ make a referral only after changes to improve performance have been documented.

Prevention – The act of stopping something from happening; in RtI, a multi-level prevention system is established to address identified areas of risk for individual students in order to stop academic or social failure and avoid the potential for identification as a student with a disability.

Primary Prevention Level – The first level in a multi-level prevention system. It consists of high quality core curriculum and researched-based instructional practices that meet the needs of most students. It may also be referred to as the core curriculum or universal strategies.

Problem-Solving Model – Within an RtI, or PBIS model, a problem-solving model is used to tailor an intervention for an individual student. A problem-solving approach typically has five stages: problem identification, problem analysis, plan, implementation, and plan evaluation.

Progress Monitoring – Used to assess a student's performance in order to quantify her or his rate of improvement or responsiveness to intervention, to adjust the student's instructional program to make it more effective and suited to the student's needs, and to evaluate the effectiveness of the intervention. Progress monitoring can be implemented with individual students or an entire class.

Progress Monitoring Probes – Individual assessment given to a student by the teacher, usually weekly, to provide on-going information about a student's performance and response to instruction and intervention over time.

Promising Practices – Includes practices that were developed based on theory or research, but for which an insufficient amount of original data have been collected to determine the effectiveness of the practices. Practices in this category may have been studied, but not using the most rigorous study designs.

Pullout – A program that takes students out of the regular classroom during the typical school day and places them in an alternative program or setting for services.

Pyramid – The RtI pyramid or triangle shows the expected model of teachers being able to meet the needs 80% of students in their classrooms with effective Primary Prevention; 15% of student needs may be met through strategic interventions, and 5% may require intensive intervention.

Questionable Progress – Comparison of the *trendline* to the *aimline* on a progress monitoring graph shows improvement, with those reviewing the data unsure if continuation of the intervention will result in the desired goal. Decisions for this type of progress may be to continue for a set time and re-assess or follow the choices for making poor progress.

Random Acts of Improvement – Are what result when there is not a focused approach or shared vision.

Referral – Request made from one level of team to another for consideration of specialized services such as Title, ELL, Special Education, or other services with eligibility criteria.

Reliable/reliability – The extent to which an experiment, test, or any measuring procedure consistently measures what it claims to measure. Simply put, the test will yield the same result on repeated administrations- over time and/or across test administrators.

Response to Intervention (RtI) – Integrates assessment and intervention within a multi-level prevention system to maximize student achievement and reduce behavior problems. With RtI, schools identify students at risk for poor learning outcomes, monitor student progress, provide evidence-based interventions and adjust the intensity and nature of those interventions depending on a student's responsiveness, and identify students with learning disabilities or other disabilities.

Risk Model – Risk is "the potential for something bad, harmful, or unpleasant to happen." In RtI, the focus is on learning outcomes with identified characteristics and performance data to identify students who are likely to have bad, harmful, or unpleasant learning outcomes in order to provide timely interventions and supports to positively influence student performance.

Scaffolding – Support given to assist students in learning a skill through explicit instruction, modeling, questioning, feedback, etc., to ensure student performance. Scaffolding implies supports will gradually be withdrawn as students become more independent.

Schoolwide Positive Behavior Support (SW-PBS) – Another term used to describe PBIS (see Positive Behavior Interventions and Supports).

Schoolwide Prevention System – A structured approach to providing instruction and intervention in academic, social, or behavioral areas that are aligned with the schools vision and mission to improve student achievement.

Scientifically Based – Empirical research that applies rigorous, systematic, and objective procedures to obtain valid knowledge. This research:

- Employs systematic, empirical methods that draw on observation or experiment.
- Has been accepted by a peer-reviewed journal or approved by a panel of independent experts through a comparably rigorous, objective and scientific review.
- Involves rigorous data analyses that are adequate to test the stated hypotheses and justify the general conclusions drawn.
- Relies on measurements or observational methods that provide valid data across evaluators and observers and across multiple measurements and observations.
- Can be generalized.

Screening – A process for systematically reviewing every student to identify those who struggle to learn when provided research-based Primary Prevention that is delivered with integrity and fidelity.

Secondary Prevention Level – The second level of intensity in a multi-level prevention system. Interventions are evidence-based and focus on learning or behavior needs of students identified as at risk in the areas of learning and/or behavior. Also referred to as strategic intervention.

Specific Learning Disability (SLD) – A disorder in one or more of the basic psychological processes involved in understanding or in using language, spoken or written, that may manifest itself in the imperfect ability to listen, think, speak, read, write, spell, or do mathematical calculations; and may result from conditions such as perceptual disabilities, brain injury, minimal brain dysfunction, dyslexia, and developmental aphasia. Specific learning disability does not include learning problems that are primarily the result of visual, hearing, or motor disabilities; of intellectual disability; of emotional disturbance; or of environmental, cultural, or economic disadvantage. Specific learning disability is one of the disability categories defined in IDEA 2004. (See also, Learning Disability.)

Stages of Implementation – Recognizes putting a system of responsiveness to interventions in place as a process that includes a specified set of activities identified with sufficient detail for monitoring. Systems for RtI involve five *Stages of Implementation* –

1. Study and Commit

2. Plan

3. Build Capacity

4. Implement and Monitor

5. Continuously Improve

Standard Protocol Intervention Model – The provision of a research-validated intervention for a specific amount of time, duration and frequency (minutes per day, days per week, and number of weeks) with small groups of students having similar needs.

Strategic Intervention – Also known as Secondary Prevention; reflects evidence-based strategies and instructional or behavioral approaches delivered in small groups for students identified at risk for poor learning outcomes, typically students performing one to two grades below expected level.

Substantial Progress – Expected rate of improvement in student performance is considerable or exceeds expectations, as determined by comparing the *trendline* to the *aimline*.

Sufficient Progress – Expected rate of improvement in student performance is satisfactory when comparing the *trendline* to the *aimline*.

Tertiary Prevention Level – The most intense level of a multi-level prevention system; consists of intensive intervention for students who have severe learning or behavior needs, and may be individualized. Also referred to as intensive intervention.

Tier – Another term used to refer to each prevention level in the multi-level prevention system with Primary Prevention as Tier 1; Secondary Prevention as Tier 2; Tertiary Prevention as Tier 3.

(Note: the authors do not endorse use of the word 'tier' as it may communicate students are placed in an intervention and removed from the general classroom.)

Trajectory – The path of student learning over time often represented by a trend line on a graph and used as the basis for instructional decisions.

Transition Services – Activities including special education and related services and community participation as listed in the IEP to help student move to post-secondary options.

Trendline – A line on a graph that presents the line of best fit drawn through a series of data points. The trend line can be compared against the *aimline* to help inform responsiveness to intervention and to tailor a student's instructional program.

Universal Design for Learning (UDL) – A framework to improve and optimize teaching and learning for all people based on scientific insights into how humans learn; a set of principles that give all individuals equal opportunity to learn and access curriculum and instruction; these principles are using multiple means of representation, multiple means of action and expression, and multiple means of engagement.

Universal Screening – Assessments conducted to identify students who may be at risk for poor learning outcomes so that early intervention can occur. Screening assessments typically are brief and usually are administered with all students at a grade level. Some schools use a gated screening system, in which universal screening is followed by additional testing or short-term progress monitoring to confirm a student's risk status before intervention occurs.

Universal Strategies – The core programs and strategies provided to all students within the school building to promote successful student outcomes and prevent school failure in areas related to both academics and behaviors, but most commonly used to refer to primary level behavior strategies.

Valid/validity – Accuracy of an assessment, test, or experiment in measuring what it claims to measure. Tests must be valid, or measure what they claim to measure in order to use data from the instruments in decision making. (You will not want to make decisions about reading if the test does not actually measure reading.)

Sources:

National Center on Response to Intervention	rti4success.org
The Glossary of Education Reform	edglossary.org
National Center on Intensive Intervention	intensiveintervention.org
RTI Action Network	rtinetwork.org

REFERENCES AND RESOURCES

Bernhardt, V. L. (2013). *Data Analysis for Continuous School Improvement.* (3rd ed.). New York, NY: Routledge.

Bernhardt, V. L., & Hébert, C. L. (2009). *Response to Intervention (RtI) and Continuous School Improvement (CSI): Using Data, Vision, and Leadership to Design, Implement, and Evaluate a Schoolwide Prevention System.* New York, NY: Routledge.

Brown-Chidsey, R., & Steege, M. W. (2005). *Response to intervention: Principles and strategies for effective practice.* New York, NY: The Guilford Press.

Buffum, A., Mattos, M., & Weber, C. (2008). *Pyramid response to intervention: RTI, professional learning communities, and how to respond when kids don't learn.* Bloomington, IN: Solution Tree Press.

Buffum, A., Mattos, M., & Weber, C. (2010). The why behind RTI. *Interventions That Work,* 68(2), 10–16.

Burke, K., & Depka, E. (2011). *Using formative assessment in the RTI framework.* Bloomington, IN: Solution Tree Press.

Christ, T. J., Burns, M. K., & Ysseldyke, J. E. (November 2005). Conceptual confusion within response to-intervention vernacular: Clarifying meaningful differences. *NASP Communiqué,* 34(3).

Christenson, S. L. (2001). *Schools and families: Creating essential connections for learning.* New York, NY: Guilford Press.

Council for Exceptional Children. http://www.cec.org

Cummings, K. D., Atkins, T., Allison, R., & Cole, C. (2008). Response to intervention: Investigating the new role of special educators. *Teaching Exceptional Children,* 40(4), 24–31.

Denton, C. A., Fletcher, J. M., Anthony, J. L., & Francis, D. J. (2006). An evaluation of intensive interventions for students with persistent reading difficulties. *Journal of Learning Disabilities,* 39, 447–466.

Dorn, L. J., and Henderson, S. C. (2010). A Comprehensive Intervention Model: A Systems Approach to Response to Intervention (Chapter 4). *Successful approaches to RtI: Collaborative practices for improving K-12 literacy.* Newark, DE: International Reading Association.

DuFour, R., DuFour, R., Eaker, R., & Many, T. (2006). *Learning by doing: A handbook for professional learning communities at work.* Bloomington, IN: Solution Tree Press.

DuFour, R., DuFour, R., & Eaker, R. (2004). *Whatever it takes: How professional learning communities respond with kids don't learn.* Bloomington, IN: Solution Tree Press.

Explicit Direct Instruction (EDI). http://www.dataworks.ed-com

Fisher, D., & Frey, N. (2010). *Enhancing RtI: How to ensure success with effective classroom instruction and intervention.* Alexandria, VA: Association for Supervision and Curriculum Development (ASCD).

Fuchs, D., & Deshler, D. D. (2007). What we need to know about responsiveness to intervention (and shouldn't be afraid to ask). *Learning Disabilities Research & Practice,* 22(2), 129–136.

Fuchs, D., Devery, M., Morgan, P. L., & Young, C. L. (2003). Responsiveness to intervention: Definitions, evidence, and implications for the learning disabilities construct. *Learning Disabilities Research & Practice,* 18(3), 157–171.

Fuchs, D., & Fuchs, L. S. (November 2009). Responsiveness to intervention: Multilevel assessment and instruction as early intervention and disability identification. *The Reading Teacher,* 63(3), 250–252.

Fuchs, D., & Fuchs, L. S. (May/June 2007). *A model for implementing responsiveness to intervention. Teaching Exceptional Children.* Arlington, VA: Council for Exceptional Children.

Fuchs, D., & Fuchs, L. S. (2006). A framework for building capacity for responsiveness to intervention. *School Psychology Review,* 35(4), 621–626.

Fuchs, D., & Fuchs, L. S. (January/February/March 2006). Introduction to response to intervention: What, why, and how valid is it? *The Reading Teacher,* 63(3), 250–252.

Fuchs, D., & Fuchs, L. S. (2006). Introduction to response to intervention: What, why, and how valid is it? *Reading Research Quarterly,* 41(1), 93–99.

Fullan, M. (2010). *All systems go: The change imperative for whole system reform.* Thousand Oaks, CA: Corwin Press.

Fullan, M. (2009). *Motion leadership: The skinny on becoming change savvy.* Thousand Oaks, CA: Corwin Press.

Fullan, M. (2007). *The new meaning of educational change* (4th ed.). New York, NY: Teachers College Press.

Grigorenko, E. L. (March/April 2009). Dynamic assessment and response to intervention: Two sides of one coin. *Journal of Learning Disabilities,* 42(2), 111–132.

Grigorenko, E. L., & Hollenbeck, A. F. (2007). From IDEA to implementation: A discussion of foundational and future responsiveness-to-intervention research. *Learning Disabilities Research & Practice,* 22(2), 137–146.

Guskey, T. R. (1999). *Evaluating professional development.* Thousand Oaks, CA: Corwin Press.

Hall, S. L. (2008). *Implementing response to intervention.* Thousand Oaks, CA: Corwin Press.

Hargreaves, A., & Shirley, D. L. (2009). *The fourth way: The inspiring future for educational change.* Thousand Oaks, CA: Corwin Press.

Hattie, J. (2012). *Visible learning for teachers: maximizing impact on learning.* New York, NY: Routledge.

Hattie, J., & Timperley, H. (2007). The power of feedback. *Review of Education Research* (77), 81–112.

Hill, P., & Crévola, C. (1998). Evaluation of a whole school approach to prevention and early intervention in literacy. *Journal of Education for Students Placed at Risk,* 3(2), 133–157.

Howard, M. (2009). *RtI from all sides: What every teacher needs to know.* Portsmouth, NH: Heinemann.

Jennings, M. J. (2008). *Before the special education referral: Leading intervention teams.* Thousand Oaks, CA: Corwin Press.

Jenson, E. (2009). *Teaching with poverty in mind: What being poor does to kids' brains and what schools can do about it.* Alexandria, VA: Association for Supervision and Curriculum Development (ASCD).

Jimerson, S. R., Burns, M. K., & VanDerHeyden, A. M. (2007). *Response to intervention: The science and practice of assessment and intervention.* New York, NY: Springer Science+Business Media.

Johnson, E., Mellard, D. F., Fuchs, D., & McKnight, M. A. (2006). *Responsiveness to intervention (RTI): How to do it.* Lawrence, KS: National Research Center on Learning Disabilities.

Johnson, R. S., & LaSalle, R. A. (2010). *Data strategies to uncover and eliminate hidden inequities: The wallpaper effect.* Thousand Oaks, CA: Corwin Press.

Kaufman, M. J., & Lewis, L. M. Confusing each with all: A policy warning. In R. Gallimore, R., Bernheimer, L. P., MacMillan, D. L., Speece, D., & Vaughn, S. (Eds.). (1999). *Developmental perspectives on children with high-incidence disabilities.* Mahwah, NJ: Lawrence Erlbaum Associates.

Kedro, M. J. (2004, April). Coherence: When the puzzle is complete. *Principal Leadership,* 4(8), 28–32.

Killion, J. (2008). *Assessing impact: Evaluating staff development* (2nd ed.). Thousand Oaks, CA: Corwin Press.

Maise, M. (2005). *Capacity Building.* Eduflow. Retrieved from https://edulflow.wordpress.com

Marsh, J. A., Pane, J. F., & Hamilton, L. S. (2006). *Making sense of data-driven decision making in education. Evidence from Recent RAND Research.* RAND Occasional Papers. Retrieved from: http://www.rand.org/pubs/occasional_papers/2006/RAND_OP170.pdf

Marzano, R. J. (2004). *Building background knowledge for academic achievement: Research on what works in schools.* Alexandria, VA: Association for Supervision and Curriculum Development (ASCD).

Marzano, R., McNulty, B., & Waters, T. (2005). *School leadership that works: From research to results.* Alexandria, VA: Association for Supervision and Curriculum Development (ASCD).

Marzano, R., Pickering, D., & Pollock, J. (2001). *Classroom instruction that works: Researched-based strategies for increasing student achievement.* Alexandria, VA: Association for Supervision and Curriculum Development (ASCD).

Mastropieri, M., & Scruggs, T. (2005). *Effective instruction for special education.* (3rd ed.). Upper Saddle River, NJ: Pearson Allyn & Bacon.

McCarney, S. B., & Wunderlich, K. C. (2006). *Pre-referral intervention manual (PRIM).* (3rd ed.). Houten, Netherlands: HES.

Mellard, D. F., & Johnson, E. S. (2007). *RTI: A practioner's guide to implementing response to intervention.* Thousand Oaks, CA: Corwin Press.

Miller, D. (2008). *Teaching with intention: Defining beliefs, aligning practice, taking action.* Portland, ME: Stenhouse Publishers.

Moss, C. M., & Brookhart, S. M. (2009). *Advancing formative assessment in every classroom: A guide for instructional leaders.* Alexandria, VA: Association for Supervision and Curriculum Development (ASCD).

National Association of State Directors of Special Education. (2006). *Response to intervention: NASDSE and CASE white paper on RtI.* Alexandria: VA: NASDSE, Inc. Retrieved from http://www.nasdse.org

National Association of State Directors of Special Education. (2008). *RtI Blueprints for Implementation for district and school.* Retrieved from http://www.nasdse.org

National Center for Learning Disabilities. http://www.ncld.org

National Mathematics Advisory Panel (U.S.). (2008). *The final report of the National Mathematics Advisory Panel.* Washington, DC: U.S. Department of Education.

National Reading Panel (U.S.), & National Institute of Child Health and Human Development (U.S.). (2000). *Report of the National Reading Panel: Teaching children to read : an evidence-based assessment of the scientific research literature on reading and its implications for reading instruction : reports of the subgroups.* Washington, D.C.: National Institute of Child Health and Human Development, National Institutes of Health.

National Center on Response to Intervention (several documents and information). http://www.rti4success.org

National Research Center on Learning Disabilities. http://www.nrcld.org

The New Teacher Project. (2015) *The Mirage: Confronting the hard truth about our quest for teacher development.* Retrieved from http://tntp.org/assets/documents/TNTP-Mirage_2015.pdf

Newmann, F., Smith, B., Allensworth, E., & Bryk, A. (2001). *School instructional program coherence: benefits and challenges.* Chicago, IL: Consortium on Chicago School Research.

Northouse, P. G. (2009). *Leadership: Theory and practice.* Thousand Oaks, CA: Sage Publications. Open Court Reading. http://www.opencourtresources.com/

O'Brien, J., Pearpoint, J., & Kahn, L. (2010). *The PATH and MAPS Handbook.* Toronto, ON: Inclusion Press.

Oxley, D. (2008). Creating Program Instructional Coherence. *Principal's Research Review,* 3(5).

Popham, W. J. (2010). *Everything school leaders need to know about assessment.* Thousand Oaks, CA: Corwin Press.

Popham, W. J. (2008). *Transformative assessment.* Thousand Oaks, CA: Corwin Press.

Reeves, D. (2006). *The learning leader: How to focus school improvement for better results.* Englewood, CO: Advanced Learning Press.

Reeves, D. (2002). *The daily disciplines of leadership.* San Francisco, CA: Jossey-Bass.

RtI Action Network, a program of the National Center for Learning Disabilities (resources and information). http://www.rtinetwork.org

Searle, M. (2010). *What every school leader needs to know about RtI.* Alexandria, VA: Association for Supervision and Curriculum Development (ASCD).

SEDL (1999–2000). *Promoting Instructional Coherence Project.* Retrieved from http://www.sedl.org/expertise/historical/pic.html

SEDL. Searchable bibliography database for resources on Educational Reform, *Coherent Teaching Practices, and Improved Student Learning.* Retrieved from http://www.sedl.org/pubs/pic02/bibintro.html

Senge, P. M. (2006). *The fifth discipline: The art & practice of the learning organization.* New York, NY: The Crown Publishing Group.

Shinn, M. R. (2007). Identifying students at risk, monitoring performance, and determining eligibility within response to intervention: Research on educational need and benefit from academic intervention. *School Psychology Review,* 36(4).

Shores, C. (2009). *A comprehensive RtI model: Integrating behavioral and academic interventions.* Thousand Oaks, CA: Corwin Press.

Shores, C., & Chester, K. (2009). *Using RtI for school improvement: Raising every student's achievement scores.* Council for Exceptional Children. Thousand Oaks, CA: Corwin Press.

Simmons, D. C., & Kameenui, E. J. (March 1996). A focus on curriculum design: When children fail. *Focus on Exceptional Children,* 28(7).

Simmons, D. C., Kuykendall, K., King, K., Cornachione, C., & Kameenui, E. J. (March 2000). Implementation of a schoolwide reading improvement model: No one ever told us it would be this hard! *Learning Disabilities Research and Practice,* 15(2), 92–100.

Smith-Mercier, J. L., Fien, H., Basaraba, D., & Travers, P. (2009). Planning, evaluating, and improving tiers of support in beginning reading. *Teaching Exceptional Children,* 41(5), 16–22.

Stiggins, R. J. (2007). *An introduction to student-involved assessment for learning.* (5th Ed.). Upper Saddle River, NJ: Prentice Hall.

Stiggins, R. J., Arter, J. A., Chappuis, J., & Chappuis, S. (2009). *Classroom assessment for student learning: Doing it right—using it well.* Boston, MA: Allyn & Bacon.

Strickland, C. A. (2009). *Professional development for differentiating instruction: An ASCD action tool.* Alexandria, VA: Association for Supervision and Curriculum Development (ASCD).

Thousand, J., Villa, R., & Nevin, A. (2015). *Differentiating Instruction.* (2nd ed.). Thousand Oaks, CA: Corwin Press.

Tomlinson, C. (2004). *How to differentiate instruction in mixed ability classrooms.* (2nd ed.). Alexandria, VA: Association for Supervision and Curriculum Development (ASCD).

United States Department of Education. (2006). Designing schoolwide programs. Retrieved from http://www.ed.gov/policy/elsec/guid/designingswpguid.doc

Walker-Tileston, D. (2011). *Closing the RTI gap: why poverty and culture count.* Blommington, IN: Solution Tree Press.

White, S. (2005). S*how me the proof! Tools and strategies to make data work for you.* Englewood, CO: Advanced Learning Press.

Wright, J. (2007). *RTI toolkit: A practical guide for schools.* Port Chester, NY: National Professional Resources; Dude Publishing.

INDEX

A

About the authors, ix–x
Acceptable progress, 96–101
Acknowledgements, xv–xvi
Aimline, 70, 79
Application opportunities, xv, 9, 20, 32, 62,
    68, 86, 91, 102, 110

B

Behavior, 61
Bernhardt, Victoria L., vii
Book study questions, xv, 9, 20, 32, 62, 68, 86,
    91, 102, 110
Build Capacity, 63–68

C

Collaborative processes, 19
Continuous school improvement (CSI)
    defined, 2
    evaluation, 93
    framework, 22–23
    relationship to RtI, 24
Continuously improve, 4, 8–9, 74, 93–102, 106
Cut point, 18, 41–42

D

Data points, 79
Data teams, 60, 78–83
Deficit versus risk model, 16–18
Documentation, 83–84

E

Effective classroom practices, 72–73
Effectiveness of intervention, 79–83
Evidence-based interventions, 18
Example daily schedule
    elementary, 76
    high school, 77

F

Focused acts of improvement, 30–31
Functional behavior assessment (FBA), 15

G

Glossary, xvi, 111–121

H

Hébert, Connie L., viii
How are our students doing? 28–29
**How are we going to get to where we want
    to be?** 21–23, 31–32
How did we get to where we are? 21–23, 30
How do we do business? 27–28
**How to use tools in RtI Implementation
    Guide,** 34

I

Implement and Monitor, 64–86
Implementation Integrity and Fidelity, 19
Instructional coherence, 28, 66–67
**Instructional design for primary
    prevention,** 71–73
**Instructional design for secondary and
    tertiary prevention,** 73–75
Integrity and fidelity of implementation,
    2–3, 19, 93–95
Intended audience, xii
Is acceptable progress being made? 96–101
**Is RtI being implemented with integrity
    and fidelity?** 93–95
Is what we are doing making a difference?
    21–23, 32

L

Leaders and leadership structures, 64–65
**Looking across the multiple measures of
    data,** 29

M

Monitoring implementation, 84–85
Multi-level prevention system, 11, 13–14,
  46–54
  primary prevention, level one, or core
    instruction, 46–48, 99
  secondary prevention, level two, or strategic
    intervention, 49–51, 100
  tertiary prevention, level three, or intensive
    intervention, 52–54, 101
Multiple measures of data, 24–25
Multi-Tier System of Support (MTSS),
  xiii, 12

N

**National Center on Response to
  Intervention,** 12
New in this edition, xiii–xiv

O

**Our School's System of Response to
  Intervention,** 37–38

P

Parent involvement, 67–68
PATH process, 89–90
Phaseline, 79
**Planning with the RtI implementation
  guide,** 33–62
Preface, xi–xiv
Primary prevention, 13–14, 46–48
Problem solving, 73–75
Professional learning, 65–66
Progress monitors, 44–45, 96, 98, 104
Purpose of this book, xi

R

Random acts of improvement, 30–31
Recommendations, 109
References and Resources, xvi, 123–128
Referral processes and documentation, 19,
  60–61
Relationship of CSI to RtI, 24

Response to Intervention (RtI)
  applying behavior, 61
  components of, 18–19, 39–45
    schoolwide assessment inventory, 39–40
    universal screeners, 41–43
    progress monitor, 44–45
  core principles, 15–16
  cycle of activities, 69
  data teams, 60, 78–83
    substantial progress, 80
    sufficient progress, 81
    questionable progress, 82
    poor progress, 82
  defined, 1
  impact, 102
  implementation and monitoring timeline, 87–91
  implementation guide, 18–19, 33–62, 64, 87–90,
    93–94, 96, 102, 109
  intent, 16
  other related items for which to plan, 61
  relationship to special education, 20
  support protocol, 59
  system, 11–12
  team, 57–58
  what it is not, 106–108
Roles and responsibilities, 55–60
  RtI team, 57–58
RtI and CSI, 1–9
RtI Implementation Guide
  www.routledge.com/cw/bernhardtandhebert

S

Schoolwide assessment inventory, 39–40
Schoolwide prevention system, 67
Screening assessments, 18
Secondary Prevention, 13–14, 49–51
Sharing with staff, 65
Special Education
  Relationship to RtI, 20
Stages of implementation, xiii, 3–9, 104–106
  Stage 1: study and commit, 4–5, 104
    purpose of, 5
    key activities, 5
  Stage 2: plan, 4, 6, 104
    purpose of, 6
    key activities, 6
  Stage 3: build capacity, 4, 7, 63–65, 105
    purpose of, 7
    key activities, 7

Stage 4: implement and monitor, 4, 7–8, 69,
　　105–106
　　purpose of, 8
　　key activities, 8
Stage 5: continuously improve, 4, 8–9, 74, 106
　　purpose of, 9
　　key activities, 9
Standard protocol, 73–75
Structure of this book, xii–xiv
Summary and conclusions, 103–110
Support Protocol, 59

T

Table of contents, v–vii
Tertiary Prevention, 13–15, 52–54
Trendline, 70, 79

U

Universal design for learning, 72, 86
Universal screeners, 41–43, 97, 103
Universal strategies, 18

W

What are our processes? 29
**What is the impact of RtI
　　implementation?** 102
Where are we now? 21–24
　　how are our students doing? 28–29
　　how do we do business? 27–28
　　what are our processes? 29
　　who are we?, 26
Where do we want to be? 21–23, 30–31
Who are we? 26

Lightning Source UK Ltd.
Milton Keynes UK
UKHW050236080122
396800UK00005B/65